Advance Praise for
Building Health-Promoting
Organizations

"Suzy Harrington offers a well-written, engaging, and thoughtful view of workplace health and the role of chief wellness officers in championing these efforts. She intertwines historical and contemporary events with colorful and humorous anecdotes. She emphasizes the importance of purpose and culture—two critical pillars in establishing best-in-class health-promotion programs. Most importantly, she spotlights measurement and evaluation—not just as nice-to-haves, but as critical elements for the long-term sustainability of initiatives. To build and maintain excellent programs, you need credible data, analysis, and interpretation—to tell data-driven stories that your audiences understand and buy into. Suzy's model helps leaders track what truly matters, linking culture change to tangible results."

— **Ron Goetzel, PhD**
Senior Scientist, Johns Hopkins University;
Director, Institute for Health and Productivity Studies

"Dr. Harrington elevates the conversation on well-being from individual behavior to organizational design. Centering on purpose, she shows that an organization with a strong WHY can manage any HOW. This book is a practical guide for anyone interested in creating a flourishing organization."

— **Vic Strecher, PhD, MPH**
University of Michigan; Founder, Kumanu, Inc.

"This book ends with a pithy bit of wisdom: 'This work is messy. It's powerful. It's personal.' For the reader's benefit, every preceding page provides *clarity* to help with the messy; ideas and tools to *enhance* your power as an activator (or leader) for workplace well-being; and practical make-it-happen guidance so you can truly personalize your own strategy for culture change. The Harrington Well-Being Model draws from years of experience, case examples, and research on what works for healthy culture change. Everyone talks about culture as the center point for effective health promotion. The elegance of this model (Why, Who, What, How, and When) shows you exactly how to do it. Rotate the rings!"

— **Joel B. Bennett, PhD, CWP**
President, Organizational Wellness & Learning Systems (OWLS);
Author, *Well-Being Champions: A Competency-Based Guidebook*

"Too often, books try to tell us *what* to do, as if actions alone are enough. This book equips leaders to go beyond checklists of items to the *why* and *how* that build sustainable culture change. Suzy gives readers value through a refreshing mix of storytelling and rigor."

— **Wendy D. Lynch, PhD**
Founder, Analytic-Translator.com

"Dr. Suzy Harrington has written the playbook every well-being leader has been waiting for. *Building Health-Promoting Organizations* transforms complex systems into clear, actionable pathways that make real change possible. It's both a map and a call to courage for those of us committed to building cultures where people and purpose thrive."

— **Anna Fitch Courie, DNP, RN, PHNA-BC**
Founder, Built Well Consulting; Chief Well-Being Officer,
Clemson University

"Well-being isn't just about programs and services—it's about creating a culture of care, improving the way the work gets done, and leading system-wide transformations. In her phenomenal book *Building Health-Promoting Organizations*, Suzy Harrington shows us how we can. For any wellness leader who has struggled to get workplace wellness to work and is seeking a better way, here's your indispensable guide. I cannot recommend this book enough!"

— **Laura Putnam**
CEO & Founder, Motion Infusion;
Author, *Workplace Wellness that Works*

"Strong leadership relies on the scaffolding of clarity and compassion. Dr. Harrington's model provides exactly that, giving leaders a framework to transition from good intentions to systemic culture change. It is a valuable contribution to the fields of leadership and well-being."

— **Renee Moorefield, PhD**
CEO, Wisdom Works Group, Inc.

"Wow—Dr. Harrington's book is amazing! She has taken the elusive concept of employee well-being and created a framework that serves as a road map to true cultural change. It provides tools and practical guidance to guide those working in this vital space. She has nailed the essence of the issue and provided structure for a true solution. I can't wait to share it with all the CWOs and those in my network. Bravo!"

— **Mary Gallagher-Seaman, MSN, RN, NE-BC, GERO-BC**
Co-lead of a large-scale federal Chief Well-Being Officer program

"The pursuit of well-being is necessarily complex. I've had the privilege of learning from and with Dr. Harrington, customizing her model with teams at multiple institutions to successfully visualize that complexity and create actionable strategy. With this book, she has clearly illustrated and contextualized an accessible model for any leader ready to do the same."

— **Chris Dawe**
AVP Health & Well-Being, University of Houston

"I've always admired Suzy's gift for making complex systems accessible. This book captures that same spirit—clear, practical, and motivating for anyone ready to lead change."

— **Christine Nicodemus**
Founder & CEO, Wayhaven

"Big promises don't shift culture—aligned daily choices do. Suzy Harrington's model shows exactly how to line up purpose, people, and practice so small acts add up. From upstream prevention to policy, this is how ripples become waves."

— **Paul Wesselmann, MA**
"The Ripples Guy"
Writer, Speaker, Bridge-Builder

"The current best available evidence demonstrates that effective health promotion strategies need to be holistic and address multiple determinants of health. Dr. Harrington's book helps the reader think broadly about the health of people across all facets of an organization and work to provide interventions and programs that are comprehensive and sustainable."

— **Susan M. Swider, PhD, PHNA-BC, FAAN**
Professor, Community, Systems and Mental Health Nursing,
Rush University

"Whether your career was born in well-being or you had well-being thrust upon you, Suzy Harrington's book will point you to her proven methods of program success. Chock full of real-world examples and best practices, this guide helps you ask and answer the most important wellness strategy questions for your organization."

— **Michael Grimsley, MPH, CHES, CSCS**
Corporate Wellness Specialist, Health Fitness Corporation

BUILDING HEALTH-PROMOTING ORGANIZATIONS

A Practical Model For
Making It Happen

SUZY HARRINGTON DNP, RN, MCHES

Modern Wisdom Press
Crestone, Colorado, USA
www.ModernWisdomPress.com

Copyright © Suzy Harrington, 2025

All rights reserved. No part of this publication may be reproduced or transmitted in any form or by any means, mechanical or electronic, including photocopying or recording, or by any information storage and retrieval system, or transmitted by email, without permission in writing from the author. Reviewers may quote brief passages in reviews.

Disclaimer: To protect the privacy of certain individuals, some names and identifying details have been changed. Neither the author nor the publisher assumes any responsibility for errors, omissions, or contrary interpretations of the subject matter within.

Published 2025

Paperback ISBN: 978-1-951692-55-1
E-book ISBN: 978-1-951692-56-8

Cover design by Karen Sperry
Back cover and author page photos courtesy of Dreamwave

*To all the health and well-being professionals
who work tirelessly and care deeply,
you are making it happen.*

*To the colleagues, friends, and mentors
who have walked alongside me and led the way,
thank you for showing every day that
we make a difference.*

CONTENTS

Foreword *11*

Introduction *15*

SECTION ONE
Understanding the Evolving and Complex Landscape of Health and Well-Being

Chapter 1   Purpose and Historical WHYs 27

Chapter 2   WHO Are Your People? 39

Chapter 3   Broadening the WHAT to Prioritize Whole-Person Well-Being 47

Chapter 4   Pathways That Create Well-Being Throughout the HOW 59

Chapter 5   Practices to Include the Upstream WHEN 73

SECTION TWO
Activating Your Harrington Well-Being Model

Chapter 6   Anchoring Your Purpose (WHY) 85

Chapter 7   Understanding Your People and Their Needs (WHO) 95

Chapter 8   Prioritizing Your Wellness Dimensions (WHAT) 107

Chapter 9   Creating Pathways Across Your Levels of
            Influence (HOW) 119

Chapter 10 Navigating Your Practices Through the
            Continuum of Care (WHEN) 137

Chapter 11 Assembling and Activating Your Blueprint for
            Successfully Building Your Health-Promoting
            Organization (All Together Now) 149

SECTION THREE
Making It Happen: Practical Tools for Advancing Your Health-Promoting Organization

Chapter 12 Develop Your Well-Being Team 179

Chapter 13 Use Strategic Communication
            to Transform Your Messages into Momentum 195

Chapter 14 Tell Your Story with Data to Strengthen
            Your Insight, Alignment, and Impact 221

Chapter 15 Tips from My Journey to Help You Thrive,
            Personally and Professionally 239

About the Author 255

Acknowledgments 257

Additional Resources Guide...261

Endnotes 281

Thank You 286

Foreword

I first became aware of Dr. Suzy Harrington when she introduced her model in a January 2016 article in the *American Journal of Health Promotion*. What impressed me about it at the time was its holistic, multi-disciplinary, and multi-dimensional approach to workforce well-being. Even more impressive was that the model was developed out of her work in the trenches as one of the first chief wellness officers in higher education. Unlike many published models or frameworks, hers emerged out of real-world application to align and give structure to the scattered and siloed wellness efforts at Oklahoma State University.

A few years later, we had the opportunity to meet at a professional conference and completed the first of many walk-and-talk conversations that had us swapping stories and impressions about the status of the field, the challenges we were encountering as we tried to advance evidence-based practices in workplace settings, and what changes we were contemplating in our own career paths.

In 2021, I went on sabbatical from my job leading research for a nonprofit organization devoted to advancing best practice approaches to workforce well-being. When I decided to write a book about how to address the spiritual dimension of well-being, Suzy's model was the first one that came to mind. We connected, and I learned that she'd tested and refined her original model in multiple higher education and healthcare organizations.

I included her model in my first book and invited her to present it in panel presentations at professional conferences. She also wrote a series of articles for the *American Journal of Health Promotion* about how to address spirituality as part of a comprehensive approach to workplace well-being.

As Suzy shares in the introduction, culture change is indeed hard work.

For those who have been doing this work, you may find validation and reinforcement around what you've learned works and doesn't work, and enjoy the solidarity and encouragement in these pages on how to move forward when things get stuck.

If you are new to the health-promotion field, this book serves as a fantastic primer for adopting a more strategic, science-backed, and systems-based approach. It would have been helpful to have this book as a text in my academic training more than 30 years ago.

Now that I've read a near-final version of the book, I will boldly state that you are in for a treat!

Here's why I remain a superfan of this model and why I'll be sharing this book with my professional peers.

- The Harrington Well-Being Model and the recommendations in this book are grounded in research. This means you don't have to wonder whether there is a scientific evidence base for the content. She shares her sources in the book, and she's kept abreast of the evolving thought leadership and research in the field.

- You'll gain lessons learned from Suzy's decades of experience working at all levels of organizations to put this model through its paces. She shares how the model helped her gain traction with executive leaders and align stakeholders across multiple departments and functions.

- The model is highly practical and actionable, and it is useful for strategic planning, operational assessment, program development, strategic communications development, and measurement and evaluation.

- In addition to the model, Suzy shares the tools and frameworks that have been most helpful to her as she's worked to align the often disparate well-being efforts scattered and siloed across various complex organizations.

- The Harrington Well-Being Model illuminates the necessary complexity of the hard work of culture change, and Suzy's ample stories and real-world examples are presented in a way that makes the challenge seem more approachable and feasible. The best part is that she walks the reader through how to use the model, which is often lacking in books of this type.

No matter where you are in your health-promotion journey, this book will challenge you to think boldly, expansively, and holistically. It also gives you the tools you need to share this vision and build support with the stakeholders you'll need on board to help you achieve it.

So settle in, dare to dream, and learn how to "make it happen."

— **Jessica Grossmeier, PhD, MPH**
Author of *Reimagining Workplace Well-Being: Fostering a Culture of Purpose, Connection, and Transcendence* and *Well at Work: Chart Your Course with Purpose, Connection, and Transcendence*

Introduction

When I became the first dedicated chief wellness officer (CWO) in higher education in 2013, I was exactly where you might be today—excited, hopeful, and a bit overwhelmed. I thought that if I could simply gather the current well-being programs, services, and policies, such as those offered by the recreation and wellness center, the nutritious meal options provided by food services, and the tobacco-free policy, I could just add some strategies and marketing, and everything would fall into place. But I soon realized that well-being isn't just about programs and services—it's also about infrastructure, alignment, and culture.

You are probably realizing this too. You likely picked up this book because you care deeply not only about the wellness programs you're responsible for but also about the people you work hard to empower and the communities you serve. You want to create and support a health-promoting organization—one that actively provides a comprehensive approach focused on prevention, engagement, and empowerment. And you are committed to creating environments that emphasize collaboration and ongoing improvement—ultimately promoting healthy lifestyles in a positive setting that feels good.

Regardless of where you are on your journey—whether you are a seasoned health and well-being expert, a new CWO, someone simply curious about the field, or an overworked professional who is juggling well-being responsibilities alongside other duties—it's a lot. Still you're passionate and purposeful, and perhaps also a bit overwhelmed. And you're not alone.

Across education, healthcare, business, and other sectors, talented individuals like you are delivering exceptional work, often with limited resources. But even the best efforts can feel scattered, siloed, or stagnant. Burnout and stress are rising. Budgets are tight. Priorities are ever-changing. Despite the activity, the impact isn't what we wellness professionals had hoped for, especially with the numerous conflicting directions, needs, opportunities, and shifting and competing strategies, priorities, and guidance.

You might be wondering, *Why is it like this? Is there a smarter, more connected way to do this?* Yes, there is! And I wrote this book to help you see what it looks like so you can make it happen.

It Is Complex!

Creating cultures of care is complicated, perhaps necessarily so. As I'm sure you realize, there are many components that can quickly become confusing. In this book, I'll share a proven way to see their intersectionality as they interact. The world is changing, and the role of health and well-being is evolving. I hope to empower you with information I wish I'd had when I began my journey.

Over the years, I've led system-wide transformations across academic, community, and healthcare settings, including serving as the Air Force Health Education and Fitness Program Manager; Director of Health, Safety, and Wellness at the American Nurses Association; CWO at Oklahoma State University; and Assistant Vice President for Student Health & Well-Being at the University of Houston (UH)—along with similar leadership roles at Georgia

Tech and Texas Children's Hospital, in addition to a variety of interim faculty and consulting opportunities.

In every setting, and through national consulting and speaking, I kept hearing the same questions:

- How can I connect the dots?
- How can I get everyone on board?
- How can I make this sustainable?

These questions led to the creation of the Harrington Well-Being Model©, co-developed and refined through real-world use in higher education and healthcare. It reflects what I've learned from decades of professional experience. True well-being isn't about adding more programs; it's about shifting culture. It's about transforming how organizations think, plan, collaborate, and lead. It is challenging and complex, necessarily, and it shows no signs of becoming any less so.

From Rubik's Cube to Clarity: The Birth of the Harrington Well-Being Model

I didn't set out to create a framework. Like you, I was trying to "do all the things." As I mentioned, in one of my earliest roles, I thought I could gather all the wellness programs on campus, arrange them like the bones of a skeleton, add some strategic "muscle," and voilà—transform everything.

It didn't work that way. I quickly realized that organizational well-being is more like a Rubik's Cube, with many theories, frameworks, and priorities that aren't in order. Once I started visualizing those layers as connected—constantly turning across purpose, audience, well-being topics, approaches, and timing—everything shifted. I could finally understand the complexity and vision and help others do the same.

The Harrington Well-Being Model was developed from decades of practical experience and deep engagement with various frameworks and philosophies, including the National Prevention Strategy, wellness wheels, Maslow's Hierarchy of Needs, Prochaska's Stages of Change, socio-ecological models, and public health systems. But theory alone was not enough. I needed something that could help real people engage and make meaningful decisions in complex settings—something that invited engagement, clarified choices, and guided organizations from fragmented efforts to unified action.

As the model evolved, it was shaped by years of collaboration with interdisciplinary teams—including student affairs leaders, clinicians, health educators, human resources (HR) professionals, faculty, and researchers—across campuses, hospitals, national initiatives, and professional associations. It was tested in strategic plans, team retreats, executive briefings, and program design, and has since been successfully adopted by organizations far and wide. Each iteration strengthened and refined it.

Today, the model is represented by concentric rotating rings. At the center is the WHY—your shared purpose and values. Surrounding that are the rings that represent each of the following elements.

- **WHO - People:** The people and audiences you serve
- **WHAT - Priorities:** The dimensions of well-being

- **HOW - Pathways:** The strategies and levels of influence grounded in the Socio-Ecological Model
- **WHEN - Practices:** The timing and scope across the continuum of care, from promotion and prevention to risk reduction, intervention, and recovery

The rings rotate because real life isn't linear. Wellness work is dynamic, adaptable, and constantly changing. These rings also intersect, much like people, programs, and systems do. The model is designed to reflect that movement and interconnectedness. It doesn't eliminate complexity, but it helps you navigate it with structure, vision, and shared language.

Because it was designed to be practical and applicable, the framework works across various sectors: from higher education to healthcare and from leadership retreats to frontline operations. You'll find it useful in planning, communicating, evaluating, and ultimately guiding your next steps.

What You Can Expect from the Model and This Book

The results from implementing the Harrington Well-Being Model have been game-changing, helping dedicated well-being pros like you (and me) find clarity in the chaos. When you utilize my framework, you will be able to…

- Transform wellness from scattered programs into a cohesive, strategic movement.
- Align loosely coordinated well-being efforts around a shared language, purpose, and priorities.

- Engage with leadership to foster commitment and support.
- Empower frontline teams to turn ideas into action.
- Embed well-being into the core of culture, operations, and policy.

I wrote this book for you, my well-being colleague. Your title and/or professional background might be that of a health educator, nurse, social worker, counselor, healthcare provider, or human resources professional. Or you may come from an entirely different field. The setting you work in could be a corporate environment, healthcare, higher education, state or city public health, or something completely different. There is no single path, but what connects us all is that we share a passion for well-being.

As I began writing, I pictured you as someone I could speak to directly. This led me to think about the leaders I've worked with and admired, along with their successful qualities: bold vision, strategic thinking, and the ability to get things done. To make you "real" as I wrote, I wanted to name you, so I came up with alliterative pairs such as Visionary Velma/Victor, Strategic Sally/Sam, and Mollie/Mike Make-It-Happen.

Mollie/Mike Make-It-Happen resonated the most, as you are truly doing just that—making it happen! You're ready to roll up your sleeves, full of energy and purpose. To make it happen, you likely also have a clear vision and strategy. That's how the title of the book, *Building Health-Promoting Organizations: A Practical Model for Making It Happen*, came about—because you are genuinely making it happen!

My degree is a Doctor of Nursing Practice (DNP) with a focus on the business and leadership aspects of healthcare. It's rooted in applied and implementation science—translating research into action, outcomes, and real-world impact. My goal is to provide you with clear, proven strategies—derived from decades of leadership experience and supported by both research and practical application. This book aims to help you make informed, effective, and compassionate decisions—and to lead your work with clarity, confidence, and purpose.

Toward that end, I've organized it into three sections:

- **Section One** provides an overview of the problem, including a historical perspective on why the traditional approach to well-being is neither strategic nor effective—and why it's time to reimagine wellness programs as well-being systems, to set the stage for the development of your well-being model.

- **Section Two** presents the solution—the Harrington Well-Being Model—with a detailed focus on the five core aspects (the "rotating rings"). It explains how this approach simplifies complexity, promotes alignment, supports meaningful change from an operational perspective, and helps you create your version.

- **Section Three** helps you "make it happen" by providing additional tools, strategies, and inspiring examples for your own professional self-care to engage stakeholders, align work and strategic communication, tell your story with data, and transform and sustain progress.

Some of what you'll read may feel familiar and reassuring. Other parts might challenge long-held beliefs or prompt you to think in new ways. That is intentional. Growth often requires both learning and unlearning. What I know for sure is that you are already doing the work. You are showing up. You care. You believe in something better. I hope this book provides you with the tools, clarity, and courage to lead well-being conversations with even more impact, alignment, and joy. My hope is that this journey is as transformative as it is informative. To help ensure it is, I've added reflective exercises at the end of each chapter in a section called "Make It Yours! Make It Happen!" So grab a notebook, create a fresh document in your favorite digital notetaker, or whatever method works best for you—because I hope to guide you to think more critically, strategically, and actionably about how you can make extraordinary things happen.

Finally, a quick note: Many of the examples I share come from higher education or healthcare, as those are the sectors I know best, but they're intended to spark your own creativity and help you see how these concepts can apply to your unique organization and context.

Let's keep making it happen…together.

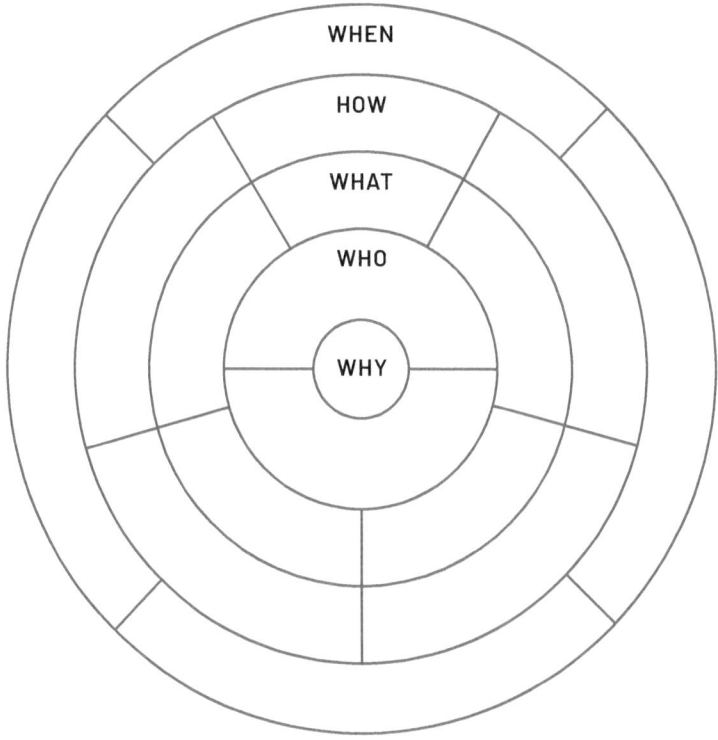

Figure 0.1: *The Basics of the Harrington Well-Being Model*

SECTION ONE

UNDERSTANDING THE EVOLVING AND COMPLEX LANDSCAPE OF HEALTH AND WELL-BEING

WELL-BEING IS NOT JUST AN INITIATIVE; IT IS A CULTURE. Health-promoting organizations don't arise from a single program or department but from coordinated, multifaceted efforts rooted in purpose, strategy, and meaningful connections. However, complexity doesn't have to cause confusion.

In this section, you'll explore how the landscape of health and well-being has evolved—shifting from clinical intervention to prevention, and now toward systems thinking and upstream strategies. You'll also learn about the main drivers of change over the decades. To illustrate this evolution, I'll explain how my professional journey has followed a similar path. And finally, you'll be introduced to the five dimensions of the Harrington Well-Being Model—WHY, WHO, WHAT, HOW, and WHEN—laying the groundwork for your journey to make amazing things happen for improved health and well-being for your organization and the people it serves.

CHAPTER 1

Purpose and Historical WHYs

Let's start this journey together by taking a trip back to 1986, when I began my career as an Air Force nurse, later shifting to other hospital-based clinical nursing roles, such as intensive care. This was the perfect example of the conventional service model—helping people one-on-one within the larger medical framework. However, when I served as a school nurse, everything changed. There I educated students and staff about healthy behaviors, nutrition, and the importance of physical activity.

I still smile thinking about a one-room rural schoolhouse where I used a pig's heart and a syringe to demonstrate how blood flows through the chambers. It was messy and memorable, and it sparked a love for prevention. Critically, I realized I wanted to stop illness before it began.

This led me to pursue a master's in health services and wellness in 2001. (Keep in mind that "wellness" wasn't a mainstream idea at that point, but it was starting to get some attention.) After completing my degree, I continued to explore health education and prevention in roles across Air Force Health and Wellness Centers, national nonprofits, and later the American Nurses Association (ANA), focusing on preventing chronic illnesses such as cardiac disease, hypertension, and diabetes by educating people on preventive health behaviors. This education concentrated on the physical aspects of nutrition and activity to lower blood pressure and stabilize blood sugar and cholesterol levels. We emphasized the importance of caring for our health, much like we do with our cars or teeth, through regular preventive screenings.

These jobs revealed a powerful truth: Individual behavior change is important, but without supportive environments, sustainable well-being remains unattainable. If the culture doesn't allow people to take vacations, if vending machines only offer junk food, or if someone lives in a food desert—and if policies or culture don't make the healthy choice the easy choice—how can anyone truly thrive?

That realization deepened my focus. I earned a Doctor of Nursing Practice (DNP) degree in 2006, with a focus on business and leadership in healthcare, specifically in health promotion and population health.

What Plagued Wellness

Everywhere I turned, people had preconceived ideas about what wellness should be. For some, it meant more yoga. Others thought wellness carts or resilience posters were the answer. Clinical teams saw it as disease management.

This misalignment in understanding wellness can often be one of our biggest challenges. Many of these efforts were valuable, but they were often disconnected. They lacked a unifying strategy and were often limited to the physical realm, even though mental health became a hot topic. That's the core challenge: Systemic problems can't be solved with feel-good programs alone. True well-being requires upstream thinking, cross-sector collaboration, and systems-level change. It means understanding wellness not just as a set of programs but also as a culture and a strategic priority. And culture change is difficult. People often say they want change, but then resist the shifts needed to achieve it.

I experienced this firsthand when I took on the job that I believed would be my career pinnacle: becoming the first dedicated CWO in higher education at Oklahoma State University. I was eager to apply everything I had learned in practice. I thought our WHY was clear—we wanted people to be healthy. But that meant different things to different people. The president's priority was for prospective employers to view our graduates as healthy, well-rounded, and ready to contribute without increasing their future healthcare costs. The staff sought easier access to nutritious food. The faculty longed for solutions to chronic stress and burnout. And the students? They wanted to have fun, succeed, and learn without feeling overwhelmed.

I was overwhelmed almost immediately. The needs were enormous and the silos deep.

Each group had a valid point. Each held a piece of the puzzle. But without a shared purpose to unite them, we were scattering our efforts instead of amplifying our impact. When I asked my university president what to prioritize, he smiled and said, "All of it." Not exactly clarifying. That's when I realized our first step wasn't another program—it was getting clear on *why* we were doing any of it in the first place.

> Purpose is your guiding star, keeping you grounded amid complexity and pushing you forward with clarity. Let it lead you to your next step.

Why Start with WHY?

Every successful well-being strategy starts with a clear and compelling sense of purpose, a reason for being. It is the "why we do what we do," the heartbeat behind the programs we launch and the cultures we aim to build. Without a well-defined why, even the most beautifully designed initiatives can feel scattered, short-lived, and disconnected. A strong vision provides clarity, energizes teams, and guides direction. It influences what you do…or don't do. Getting the right WHY helps you reach your goals, acting as a road map. It transforms effort into momentum.

When I started developing the Harrington Well-Being Model, I placed WHY at its core, the literal and metaphorical bullseye. Later, a colleague shared Simon Sinek's best-selling book *Start with Why: How Great Leaders Inspire Everyone to Take Action*.[1] It confirmed what I had always felt: Purpose drives impact. As he explains: "People don't buy what you do; they buy why you do it."

Purpose attracts, aligns, and sustains. But too often in health and well-being, we jump straight into doing—launching programs, offering services, and implementing quick fixes without pausing to connect to WHY.

Let's illustrate this with two short stories.

Blockbuster, the once-dominant video-rental chain, thrived for years by selling access to videos. But when Netflix entered the scene with a clear and visionary goal—to make entertainment accessible and personalized—Blockbuster failed to evolve. The company's WHY was tied to a product, not a mission. And when the world changed, it couldn't adapt. It wasn't about entertainment; it was about tapes on shelves.

Now compare that with Starbucks. At its core, it isn't just selling coffee; it's building a community. Their mission? "To be the premier purveyor of the finest coffee in the world, inspiring and nurturing the human spirit—one person, one cup, and one neighborhood at a time."[2] That clear purpose guides everything they do, from training staff to designing their spaces. It's why people choose Starbucks or other coffee shops, even when they can brew their coffee at home.

So as you explore the WHY of health and well-being, you must ask yourself: "Am I designing initiatives like Blockbuster—

focused on activities and outputs? Or am I creating a culture more like Starbucks, one that emphasizes a deeper impact and shared meaning?"

Tracing the Evolution of WHY in Health and Well-Being

Our understanding of health and our motivation to pursue it have undergone significant changes over time. Let's take a quick walk through history to see how far we've come—and why our WHY must continue evolving.

Survival and Safety: In early human history, health focused on survival. The WHY was clear: Avoid danger, find food and shelter, and live another day. These priorities align with the basic levels of Maslow's Hierarchy of Needs, specifically physiological and safety needs.[3] There was no time for deep thinking about existence, and few lived long enough to experience what we now call a midlife crisis. Survival was the primary goal; thriving would come later.

Our stress response—fight, flight, or freeze—was designed for this. While saber-toothed tigers no longer walk our streets, our nervous systems still react to threats, like stressful emails or constant demands, as if we're fleeing from predators. Our ancient physiology doesn't always align with modern pressures.

Safety in numbers was also crucial. Our social well-being was based on tribe and a sense of belonging. These instincts continue to influence our need for connection and safety today.

Physical Health and Cleanliness: Jump ahead to ancient Greece and Rome. Health began to be viewed as more than a matter of divine will; it was something that human actions could influence. The Greeks initiated the Olympic Games in 776 BC to encourage physical fitness and reduce injuries.[4] Around 400 BC, Hippocrates, known as the Father of Medicine, emphasized the importance of balance, lifestyle, and ethics in healing at his medical school.[5] Many of his achievements still influence medicine today. We owe thanks to Rome for recognizing the link between cleanliness and health around 300 BC, developing aqueducts to supply fresh, clean water, public baths for hygiene, latrines for waste containment, and drainage systems to remove stagnant water that could harbor disease over the following 500 years.[6] These early initiatives laid the foundation for the health systems we have today.

A fun note: historically, the witch's broom and cat reflect real practices—community healers used a household broom for cleanliness, and kept cats as mousers for rodent (and disease) control.

Safety, Chronic Illness, and ROI: Closer to home, the Industrial Revolution, a period marked by industrial growth and urbanization, emphasized the need for public health and infrastructure improvements to combat overcrowded living conditions and poor sanitation. Regulations on workers' safety and health emerged in response to hazardous working conditions, where employees, including children, were forced to endure long hours in unsafe environments, often leading to injury and death, due to a lack of safety standards. Safety once again became a priority.[7]

In the workplace, efforts to promote a safety culture aimed to reduce accidents and injuries, while also boosting productivity.[8] At the same time, scientists and healthcare workers promoted the acceptance of the germ theory, developed disease-preventing vaccines and lifesaving antibiotics, and acute deaths from disease and injury began to decline.

As businesses and healthcare efforts focused on preventing injury and death, we started living longer. However, chronic diseases began to increase, along with healthcare costs. Tobacco use and poor diet/physical inactivity remained the leading causes of death,[9] and tobacco settlements occurred. The fast-food culture—with its emphasis on low-cost (highly processed) meals and supersized portions[10]—had become deeply ingrained in American life. The costs of smokers' health and the dangers of secondhand smoke were recognized, because smoke could not be contained in small sections of airplanes or airports, just as chlorine cannot be contained in a section of a swimming pool. Even nonsmokers who lived or worked with smokers were adding to healthcare expenses.[11]

Providing care for those with chronic illnesses costs significantly more in money, time, and quality of life. Employee health emerged as a result of trying to minimize the cost and burden of death, injuries, and chronic disease, as individuals often necessitate expensive care and missed time at work. The WHY continued to be an economic consideration: healthier workers missed fewer days, filed fewer claims, and cost less to insure.

This marked the beginning of the return on investment (ROI) era, where savings measured the value of wellness. Programs aimed to reduce medical and pharmaceutical costs, minimize short-term disability and workers' comp claims, lower absenteeism and reduce sick days, and decrease turnover. Wellness activities were assessed to determine if they saved money.

From Risk Reduction to Human Flourishing

But cost savings aren't the whole story. In 1948, the World Health Organization offered a radical definition: "Health is a state of complete physical, mental, and social well-being and not merely the absence of disease or infirmity."[12] This aspirational shift, from fixing to flourishing, invited a broader view of health.

Unfortunately, our systems were slow to adapt. We mainly focused on pathogenic issues and the medical model of health, which emphasizes diagnosing and treating disease and considers health as the absence of illness. Over time, however, the salutogenic approach began to gain popularity, pioneered by Aaron Antonovsky in 1979.[13] The term comes from the Latin words *salus*, meaning health, and *genesis*, meaning origin. (Think *salud* in Spanish or *salute* in Italian, both of which mean "to your health" when toasting drinks.) Salutogenesis redefines health as a continuum—not something you simply have or lack, but something that is fostered through connection, meaning, and possibility—a range from ease to dis-ease.

Salutogenesis vs Pathogenesis

	SALUTOGENESIS - UPSTREAM	PATHOGENESIS - DOWNSTREAM
LATIN DERIVATIVE	Origins/birth of health	Origins/birth of disease
FOCUS	Health creation and promotion	Disease and illness prevention
APPROACH	Holistic and proactive	Reductionist and reactive
VIEW OF HEALTH	Health as a continuum	Health as absence of disease
GOAL	Enhance well-being and "living"	Eliminate disease and risk factors
ROLE OF STRESSORS	Stressors are part of life; focus on resilience	Stressors are harmful; focus on elimination
KEY CONCEPTS	Flourish and thrive	Risk factors and pathology
OUTCOMES MANAGEMENT	Focus on positive health and quality of life	Focus on disease outcomes and symptoms

Table 1.1: Salutogenesis vs. Pathogenesis

Ron Goetzel, a scientist at Johns Hopkins, and other public health leaders have shifted the focus from ROI to value on investment (VOI), addressing this salutogenic approach, assessing wellness by its effects on morale, engagement, satisfaction, and team culture—living to work, not working to live.[14] It has become less about the bottom line and more about how we thrive. This change elevates our purpose to be further up Maslow's Hierarchy of Needs to levels of love and belonging, esteem, and the peak of self-actualization, which is the process of growing and fulfilling one's full potential.[15]

Public Health and Policy Shifts

Throughout the 2000s and 2010s, public health also embraced a broader perspective. The Institute of Medicine's Crossing the Quality Chasm urged system redesign and a strong focus on building a culture of quality. The Triple Aim highlighted the importance of population health. The Affordable Care Act emphasized the importance of prevention and equity. Preventive screenings were included in coverage. From a clinical perspective, patient-centered care became a key focus. The Department of Health and Human Services (HHS) National Prevention Strategy provided a comprehensive plan, and a round graphic (which was the impetus to developing the model for our work), to improve the health and well-being of Americans by prioritizing prevention and wellness.

So What's Your WHY Today?

Today, your purpose in health and well-being must go beyond merely fixing problems or reducing risks, beyond meeting basic physical needs or simply surviving. Your WHY is about human potential—helping individuals and communities thrive, find purpose, live according to their values, and experience joy. It's about building organizations where well-being is not just an initiative but also a way of being—woven into our culture, decisions, and shared commitments. Just as many industries now promote safety or quality as core values, a culture of well-being requires clarity, intention, and a shared sense of purpose.

Make It Yours…Make It Happen!

Your WHY serves as your compass—it keeps your well-being efforts aligned with your organization's broader mission while fueling your personal motivation. A clear purpose boosts credibility, reinforces commitment, and encourages action. When you understand your WHY, making decisions, gathering support, and overcoming challenges become simpler.

Clarify Your Purpose

1. **Name it.** In one sentence, what is my personal WHY for doing this work?

2. **Check alignment.** How does my purpose connect to our organization's mission, vision, and values?

3. **Spot the gap.** Where does our current work drift from our WHY, and what's one thing we can adjust this month to realign?

CHAPTER 2

WHO Are Your People?

Lately, I've been spending more time in my garden—a luxury of no longer moving every few years. And I'm struck by how plants teach us about people.

Every seed has potential. All plants need soil, sun, water, and care—but not in the same amounts. Orchids, tomatoes, and cacti thrive in different conditions, which are important to their survival. The gardener knows this and tailors their approach to ensure everything blooms and thrives.

The same applies to people. Everyone needs the basics—safety, connection, nourishment, purpose—and individuals thrive when their unique needs are met, in a cultivated garden where they can flourish. So when you think about creating a health-promoting organization, it's easy to focus on programs and services, and whether you are meeting the unique needs of your community. Well-being isn't only about what people do—like eating healthy foods, seeing doctors, or practicing yoga. It's about who they are, both individually and as a community, in the places where they live, learn, work, and play. Like the gardener, your role is to cultivate an environment where everyone thrives.

Thus the WHO is the core of your work. It's the reason behind your efforts and the people you serve and support. In the Harrington Well-Being Model, this ring sits right next to the purpose (the WHY), because once you understand your purpose, the next important step is knowing who you're serving. That means understanding your community deeply and recognizing that everyone in your organization is a stakeholder, with a goal of being happy, healthy, and thriving.

The Power of Knowing WHO

Humans and the communities they form are complex. Each person brings a different identity, culture, experiences, and needs to the table. Yet too often, well-being efforts focus on the loudest voices or the most familiar patterns. This is why it's critical that you pause and ask: "Are my colleagues and I truly seeing and serving everyone?"

Each subpopulation within your organization may need something slightly different. And without a coordinated approach, efforts can remain isolated—well-intentioned but disconnected. To create synergy and be effective, you must align purpose, values, and strategies across the entire spectrum of your population.

> See your people. When you recognize and reflect on the full humanity of your communities, well-being becomes more than just a goal—it turns into a shared experience.

Borrowing a term from marketing, a *target audience* refers to specific population segments. In public health, we must go further by ensuring our work is inclusive, accessible, and culturally relevant. We do this by focusing on who we are reaching (and not reaching) and designing intentionally.

Every setting is different, but a practical rule of thumb is that about 20% of your population will eagerly participate in wellness efforts, the "worried well" who jump in early; roughly 20% may not be ready to engage; and about 60% are in the movable middle, where your thoughtful design can make the most meaningful impact.

In any setting—whether in higher education, the workplace, or the community—it's essential to understand and honor the diversity of your audience. In colleges and universities, students, faculty, and staff each have their own distinct roles and needs, with students further categorized by factors such as academic level, living situation, or degree. In workplaces such as hospitals, segmentation can encompass a wide range of factors, including job roles, life stages, shift times, language, tenure, and cultural background. Communities are just as complex, with differences in age, income, interests, or zip codes shaping people's experiences.

Whether you're engaging with alumni, interns, commuters, or caregivers, understanding these differences is crucial to meeting people where they are—and developing strategies that are personal, relevant, and inclusive.

While tailoring strategies to specific subgroups is important, thinking systemically and inclusively is equally crucial. A simple example illustrates this key point.

Imagine a snowy morning, where a janitor begins shoveling the stairs leading to the school building so everyone can enter safely.

A student in a wheelchair asks, "Could you please shovel the ramp first?"

The janitor responds, "I'll get to it after the stairs."

The student gently replies, "But if you shovel the ramp first, we can all get in."

The point is not about doing more work; it's about thinking and acting differently. Clearing the ramp first takes no additional time, but it immediately benefits everyone.

Meeting Unique Needs with Thoughtful Design

So how do you serve a beautifully diverse population? One effective approach is universal design, which creates environments that accommodate the most people possible without requiring modifications.

A favorite example of mine happened at a university where I served, where all students had to take swimming lessons—a leftover requirement from a state mandate aimed at preventing drownings. We continued to offer these lessons because swimming was more than just a safety skill—it also provided social opportunities, recreation, and lifelong confidence.

But soon we realized many international female students weren't attending. After listening closely, we discovered that religious and cultural norms made co-ed lessons inaccessible. So we adapted. We offered women-only classes with privacy curtains and female instructors. The goal stayed the same, but the approach changed to meet real needs.

The takeaway? While thinking broadly, you can't always design for "the employee" or "the student" as a one-size-fits-all solution. Like shoveling the ramp, it's not about working harder—it's about a different deliberate approach that goes beyond what you usually do. Real impact happens when you meet people where they are and collaborate on solutions.

Relatedly, I would be remiss if I didn't mention something about social justice and equity. Social justice isn't always what we assume it to be. You might be familiar with the conceptual progression from equality to equity, and then to justice. A colleague once shared a drawing that I initially found powerful: It showed three children of different heights behind a fence, watching a baseball game, each standing on boxes to see over the wooden fence. In the first frame, they are all on the same number of boxes, and the shortest one still can't see over the fence (equality). The next frame shows them on different numbers of boxes, with the shortest child having the most, allowing them all to see over the fence (equity). In the final frame, the fence is completely removed (justice).[16]

But something about it made me pause. Sometimes we need the fence for safety. Maybe it should be transparent, like a chain-link fence, allowing visibility and protection. But more importantly, why are the kids behind the fence in the outfield in the first place? Why aren't they in the stands—or better yet, on the field playing?

True justice isn't just about removing barriers; it's about thinking differently. It is about redesigning the system. It asks: Who gets access? Who gets to participate? What is our WHY?

So Who's Your WHO Today?

Your WHO includes everyone within the organizational ecosystem—students, staff, faculty, employees, volunteers, and community members—each bringing unique identities, needs, and experiences. Building a health-promoting organization requires deeply understanding this diversity and designing for inclusion, not assumptions. It's about meeting people where they are, using thoughtful universal design, and ensuring every person feels valued, supported, and able to thrive. Instead of designing for the average, we design for the populations and foster conditions where all can flourish—recognizing that justice, access, and care are not just ideals but also design challenges we must intentionally address.

Make It Yours! Make It Happen!

Your WHO is the foundation of every decision you make. Understanding your audience—who they are, what they value, and what they need—turns generic wellness into meaningful, inclusive well-being strategies.

Know Your People

1. **See the whole picture.** Who are you truly serving, and who might you be missing?

2. **Check assumptions.** What beliefs (true or untested) do you hold about your population?

3. **Listen closer.** What is one step you can take this week to better understand your community's lived experience?

CHAPTER 3

Broadening the WHAT to Prioritize Whole-Person Well-Being

What comes to your mind when thinking about an organization's wellness or well-being? Chances are, it's an image of a wellness wheel with pie slices of the dimensions of wellness. These dimensions are easy to recognize and widely used, and they serve as a shared language across silos, helping to organize strategies by topic and communicate more clearly with diverse audiences.

Because words matter, people are often deeply attached to the dimensions defined by their professional organizations. I saw this firsthand during a strategic retreat with directors from the Health and Well-Being Portfolio at the University of Houston. Each specialty area—recreation, counseling, wellness, as well as health, disability, and recovery services—brought its own model. In total, we had six different wellness wheels in the room. The differences literally halted our progress.

If you've ever tried to reconcile multiple approaches, you know how elusive the WHAT can feel. A quick online search reveals thousands of wellness wheels—some with just three categories (mind, body, spirit) and others with as many as 13.

In the Harrington Well-Being Model, this wheel and its dimensions make up the WHAT ring, part of a larger and more complex framework. This ring is often the most visible and the first point of contact, because people relate to these dimensions on a personal level. Located next to the WHO ring, it creates a natural link between individuals and the organization's overall strategy. Having dimensions that resonate with your organization is crucial—they offer a shared language for alignment, engagement, and strategic focus.

Historically, well-being efforts focused on the physical dimension in such areas as exercise, nutrition, and quitting tobacco. However, today our understanding is changing. Increasing levels of anxiety, loneliness, and burnout have highlighted the importance of emotional, spiritual, and social well-being. In 2023, U.S. Surgeon General Dr. Vivek Murthy highlighted this importance in the report *Our Epidemic of Loneliness and Isolation*, emphasizing that connection is fundamental to mental and physical health.[17] He too identified five essentials for well-being, highlighting the importance of integrating social and emotional strategies into our work.

There is no universal "right" number of dimensions. Many wellness wheels include six to eight, but in my experience, starting with five—physical, emotional, spiritual, social, and professional—provides clarity and flexibility. Why five? They are easy to remember, broad enough to include diverse perspectives, and structured enough to promote cohesion. Most well-being topics fit comfortably within these categories, and they can be adapted to suit your organization's culture and priorities. When used purposefully, these dimensions help break down silos, align strategies, and foster a culture of care. Because people connect to them on a personal level, these dimensions can also become your hook, your brand, and your first point of engagement.

> The dimensions of well-being act as your bridge across silos—use them purposefully to organize, align, and inspire. Incorporate care as a fundamental part of your organization.

Harmony, Not Balance

Back to the University of Houston's strategic retreat for its Health and Well-Being Portfolio directors and our many competing wellness models. We quickly realized that what mattered most wasn't how many slices our wellness wheels had—it was how we used the dimensions to support our WHY and align with our organization's mission and values. In the end, we found a shared way forward: Our dimensions were expressed by five action-oriented words (being, doing, connecting, caring, and learning), which reflected our collective mission to work in harmony, thus creating a unifying language and helped our strategic work progress.

It is important to note that these dimensions are not silos. They are interconnected and fluid, shifting focus depending on what life (or work) demands at a given moment. A perfect illustration is college finals week. As students prioritize their academic well-being by studying and completing projects, they may neglect physical activity, sleep, or social time. Afterwards, they recalibrate.

The goal isn't balance; it's harmony. Life rarely "balances" perfectly. Instead, we humans ebb and flow, harmonizing across these dimensions. Our current challenge is to bring all these into alignment to foster human thriving.

Finally, a note on language: There's an ongoing debate about "wellness" versus "well-being." According to the World Health Organization (W.H.O.) Health Promotion Glossary of Terms (2021): "Well-being is a positive state experienced by individuals and societies. Similar to health, it is a resource for daily life and is determined by social, economic, and environmental conditions." It goes on to say this:

> Well-being encompasses quality of life, as well as the ability of people and societies to contribute to the world in accordance with a sense of meaning and purpose. Focusing on well-being supports the tracking of equitable distribution of resources, overall thriving, and sustainability. A society's well-being can be observed by the extent to which people are resilient, build capacity for action, and are prepared to transcend challenges.[18]

In short, well-being describes the outcome: the overall state of thriving and flourishing. Wellness, which isn't listed in the W.H.O. glossary, typically refers to the practices and activities that support well-being—for example, nutrition programs, fitness classes, or sleep education that nurtures physical well-being. You'll notice that I tend to use the term *well-being* more often in this book, as its core is about advancing whole-person and whole-system flourishing, rather than just individual activities. Also debated is the choice to hyphenate *well-being*; however, using it consistently is considered more important. In this book, I follow the W.H.O.'s convention by including the hyphen.

In a similar vein, the words *thriving* and *flourishing* are used in related but distinct ways. Thriving is often viewed as a process—a journey of growth, adaptation, and resilience—primarily applied to individuals. Flourishing is more often regarded as an outcome, describing a state of living or the broader collective experience of a community, culture, or organization that promotes and maintains well-being.

In essence, thriving indicates personal vitality and development, while flourishing reflects the larger shared experience. Like the terms *wellness* and *well-being*, these words sometimes overlap, and people use them differently.

Using them intentionally can enhance your message and help connect with both individual and organizational audiences. However, don't get caught up in the labels—the real focus is on maintaining an asset-based, salutogenic approach to creating the conditions where people and organizations can genuinely thrive.

Introducing the Harrington Model's Five Dimensions of Well-Being

Let me introduce the concepts behind the model's five dimensions of well-being. They are meant as a starting point for your critical thinking—your foundation, not your final destination. In Section Two, when you begin creating your own, the real strength will come from choosing descriptors or topics that genuinely resonate with your organization's culture, priorities, and audience.

For illustration, I've included the University of Houston's action words, which continue to resonate with me. At the same time, notice how these connect to more familiar and widely recognized dimensions so that you can bridge the language of your environment with these broader concepts.

Physical / Doing

This is the dimension most people immediately think of when they hear "health"—movement, nutrition, rest. But too often, it's reduced to a list of "shoulds": diet, exercise, vaccinations, and annual physicals. These words can feel like pressure, restriction, or something to start and stop rather than a sustainable way to live. Let's shift the conversation.

Instead of *diet* and *exercise*, try *nutrition* and *activity*—words that feel energizing and ongoing. They suggest a lifestyle of vitality, not deprivation. Gallup defines this dimension as "the energy to get things done,"[19] which aligns perfectly with a positive perspective of physical well-being—a foundation that fuels participation, productivity, and presence in daily life.

Emotional / Caring

Emotional well-being is often misunderstood as "mental health." When most people hear that phrase, they think about issues like stress, anxiety, or depression. Similar to the W.H.O. health definition, American sociologist Corey Keyes describes mental health as a syndrome of positive feelings and positive functioning, not just the absence of illness.[20] Emotional well-being isn't merely the absence of problems—it also includes positive feelings, coping skills, and self-awareness. It's salutogenic: health-promoting and rooted in strength. Resilience plays a role too, but I prefer to emphasize thriving and flourishing, as resilience helps us endure adversity; thriving and flourishing help us grow beyond it.

Let's be clear—emotions are not soft skills. They are essential survival skills. Emotional well-being reduces harmful coping mechanisms, builds self-efficacy, and strengthens the ability to thrive. Confidence, compassion, and self-regulation are protective tools that empower better decision-making across all areas of life. Creating environments that actively support emotional well-being is one of the most powerful ways to prevent harm and foster sustainable growth.

Social / Connecting

We are wired for connection. We thrive in community. The African concept of Ubuntu, "I am because we are," captures this truth beautifully.[21] Gallup describes it as "meaningful friendships in your life."[22] In the military, it's esprit de corps—a sense of pride, shared purpose, and mutual support.

Social well-being is the feeling that you belong, are valued, and are not alone. This is about being seen, heard, understood, valued, and appreciated. It's the friend who checks in, the group that welcomes you, and the community that lets you exhale and be seen. It's about meaningful relationships where we live, learn, work, play, and pray.

This dimension includes both informal and formal support systems. It also covers belonging and inclusion, because we thrive when we feel valued. Kindness, encouragement, and positive peer influence can be powerful drivers of healthier choices. When this dimension is broken, the effects are far-reaching.

During the early stages of the COVID-19 pandemic, the impact of social disconnection became painfully clear. It's no surprise that the International Organization for Standardization (ISO) now recognizes workplace relationships and culture as psychosocial risks (ISO 45003: Psychological Health and Safety at Work).[23] When people don't feel safe, seen, or connected, we all suffer.

Spiritual / Being

Spiritual well-being is often the quietest but most profound dimension. It's not necessarily religious, although it can be. It's about alignment and living in a way that reflects your values, purpose, and beliefs. I describe it as our sense of purpose, passion, values, and joy. It is our source of hope. It is the feeling of truly mattering.

A spiritually grounded person knows why they get out of bed in the morning. They can be present in the moment, free from regrets of the past or fears of the future. They live with clarity, rooted in what matters most.

Gallup has identified clarity of purpose as a key factor in student success.[24] Former Surgeon General Vivek Murthy has called happiness—true, deep-rooted happiness—one of the most powerful drivers of health.[25] Jessica Grossmeier, in *Reimagining Workplace Well-Being*, advocates for a culture rooted in connection, purpose, and transcendence—all spiritual concepts.[26]

Yet many workplaces avoid this dimension, fearing they may cross lines of faith or belief. But spirituality doesn't have to be divisive. You can sense it when your values match—or when they don't—with your community, team, or organization.

Spiritual well-being provides us with the strength to keep moving forward and the perspective to concentrate on what truly matters. And it's one of my personal favorites.

Professional / Learning

This dimension is often referred to by different names such as career, intellectual, or academic. I prefer *professional* because it applies to anyone at any stage of life, in any organization. We are all professionals at any level. It's about how we handle our responsibilities, pursue our goals, and make meaningful contributions to the world around us.

Gallup defines this as "liking what you do every day."[27] I'd expand that: It's about using your strengths, finding purpose in your work, continuing to grow, and experiencing a sense of progress and contribution—whether you're a student, employee, leader, or caregiver.

Professional well-being includes personal growth, lifelong learning, financial literacy, creativity, and innovation. Renee Moorefield, founder of Wisdom Works, reminds us that well leaders lead well—and professional fulfillment is a cornerstone of that ability.[28]

In our rapidly changing digital, artificial intelligence (AI)-driven world, professional well-being also involves digital literacy and adaptability. This isn't about chasing the latest app or trend—it's about building the confidence and skills to navigate a constantly evolving landscape. It means being able to identify trustworthy information, use technology to connect rather than isolate, and adapt to new tools that can enhance learning, communication, and problem-solving. As digital spaces increasingly influence our relationships, work, and even our sense of identity, these skills are not optional—they are vital for thriving as an individual and helping our community grow.

A quick note on scope: Many models treat financial well-being as its own domain rather than integrating it into Professional/Learning. Consider your organization's WHY. If addressing financial needs is central to your purpose or outcomes, elevate it as a distinct area of focus. Remember, this model is a tool, not a strict template, so adapt it to your priorities. The five dimensions I share reflect what has worked for me and often help unify different models. Use them as prompts to spark thinking and discussion, rather than as rigid categories.

A Note About Being Data-Informed

We live in an unprecedented era, where AI and other advanced technologies enable us to explore and understand complex topics in ways that challenge and broaden our assumptions. Yet as powerful as these tools are, it's crucial to pause and examine the true WHATs that influence our well-being.

For example, a 2022 survey by the American Nurses Foundation revealed an interesting gap between perception and reality.[29] While nurses reported that spending time with friends and family, enjoying leisure activities, and being in nature or around animals supported their well-being, data analysis showed stronger correlations with the following:

- Healthy nutrition
- Access to accurate information
- Connection to a spiritual community
- Practicing gratitude
- Engaging in physical activity

These insights remind us that well-being isn't just about what feels good—it's about what truly makes a measurable difference. They also highlight the importance of using data to go beyond popularity or assumptions, ensuring our strategies focus on what genuinely supports human flourishing.

So What's Your WHAT Today?

The WHAT represents the essential dimensions of well-being—physical, emotional, social, spiritual, and professional—that enable individuals and organizations to thrive and flourish. These dimensions are not isolated; they are interconnected areas of life that fluctuate based on personal and environmental factors. Although wellness models differ, having a common language around these dimensions fosters cohesion, clarity, and effective communication across departments and disciplines. More than mere checkboxes, these areas reflect what truly matters to people and offer a relatable way to engage diverse audiences. Today's view of well-being goes beyond physical health to include happiness, purpose, connection, and growth, viewing well-being as a dynamic, personalized, and holistic journey that we create together.

Make It Yours! Make It Happen!

Your WHAT determines the dimensions of well-being that you prioritize. It's not about fitting into someone else's wellness wheel—it's about choosing priorities that are meaningful, culturally relevant, and strategic for your situation.

Define Your Priorities

1. **Audit your tools.** Does your current wellness wheel or set of dimensions truly serve your people and goals?

2. **Spot the standouts.** Which dimension is most relevant right now? Which feels overlooked or under-resourced?

3. **Consider the baggage.** What professional or cultural attachments to certain dimensions or terms might help, or hinder, progress?

CHAPTER 4

Pathways That Create Well-Being Throughout the HOW

One of my first assignments for the American Nurses Association (ANA) in 2012 was to develop national standards for safe patient handling. Back then, these protocols weren't a given, and I had no idea what developing national standards would involve. However, through relationship-building, I invited national experts—an interdisciplinary team of nurses, physical therapists, and engineers—to ANA headquarters. There I saw what real systems change looks like.

These professionals came together, unpaid, without a blueprint—just driven by a shared commitment to improvement. We all understood that safe patient handling protected both patients and healthcare workers from injury. It wasn't about launching another program or having all the answers right away. It was about cultivating a shared purpose and translating it into practical, workable standards.

We quickly realized that individual responsibility alone wasn't enough; lasting change required both personal effort and organizational commitment to create safer environments.[30] That was my introduction to the importance of *how* things get done—the two-pronged approach of empowering individuals while shaping a supporting culture. I learned early that systems matter, and so do the people within them. Today, this perspective is echoed by public health leaders. In the U.S. Surgeon General's 2022 report on health worker burnout, Dr. Vivek Murthy emphasized that systemic solutions—not just individual self-care—are essential for real impact.[31]

Thus the HOW ring represents the operational layer that not only implements well-being strategies but also integrates them into the core of an organization to ensure sustainability. Along with the WHEN ring, it has the most significant influence on shifting traditional views of health and well-being. Based on the Socio-Ecological Model (SEM), this ring covers individual, interpersonal, organizational, environmental, and policy levels. These can be approached at two levels: nurturing individuals and promoting a culture of care. Although these levels may seem separate or even conflicting, their true strength comes from how they interact. Lasting change requires more than just affecting individual choices; it depends on transforming the environments, systems, structures, and cultures that shape those choices in the first place.

Historically, health strategies were reactive, focusing on treating disease through medical intervention. Over time, we shifted toward prevention by encouraging behavior change through education. Currently, we are in the next phase: recognizing that sustainable well-being depends on integrated, systems-level strategies that address both the environments where people live and the personal skills they need to manage them.

Yet too often well-being professionals depend on individual programs to accomplish what systems should support. This gap between good intentions and real change is significant. Many organizations are "*doing* healthy"—offering yoga classes, wellness fairs, or nutritious snacks—but not genuinely "*being* healthy."

As a colleague of mine often said, "How's that working out for you?"

To make well-being a lasting part of your organization, you must embed it into your strategy, operations, values, and culture. That's the core of the HOW ring: moving from fixing people to transforming culture.

> Don't just DO healthy—BE healthy. Incorporate care into your systems, culture, and strategy so well-being becomes your way of working.

Designing a Culture of Care

Have you ever heard the story about the child and the starfish?[32]

Walking along the beach one day, a child noticed hundreds of starfish stranded on the shore. Knowing they would die in the hot sun, the youngster picked them up, one by one, and tossed them back into the ocean.

A man walked by and asked, "What are you doing?"

"I'm saving the starfish," the child replied.

"You can't save them all—there are too many," the man said. "What difference can you possibly make?"

The child picked up another starfish and flung it into the sea, exclaiming, "It made a difference to that one!"

It's a heart-warming story, but it also raises some deeper questions:

Why were the starfish washing ashore in the first place?

What if we could make a systematic change so they wouldn't need saving at all?

That is why I prefer another wildlife example, one shared by Daniel Reist from the University of British Columbia. He reminds us: "If the frogs in the pond started behaving strangely, our first reaction would not be to punish them or even to treat them. Instinctively, we'd wonder what was going on in the pond."[33] The lesson is clear: Just like frogs in a pond or starfish on a beach, well-being professionals must look beyond individual struggles and focus on the environment and culture where people live, learn, and work.

It was in this spirit in 1986 that the Ottawa Charter for Health Promotion initially called for shifting health systems from focusing solely on treating illness to promoting overall well-being.[34] Its action areas—developing healthy public policies, creating supportive environments, and enhancing personal skills—formed the basis for initiatives like Healthy Cities.[35] These highlight that health is influenced by social, economic, and environmental factors beyond just clinical care.

More recently, the Geneva Charter (2021),[36] the Okanagan Charter (2015),[37] and its new companion, the Limerick Framework for Action (2025),[38] have all built upon this foundation. They call for institutions to incorporate health into every aspect of culture, while leading both local and global health-promotion efforts. These charters reaffirm the importance of creating sustainable "well-being societies" by integrating equity, environmental responsibility, and systems thinking into our operations.

These initiatives also highlight that care is more than just a feeling—it is a fundamental design principle. It must be deliberately integrated into how we organize, lead, and shape environments that help people thrive. That's why a comprehensive systems-based approach is crucial. Wellness programs alone aren't enough. We also need to reevaluate the physical spaces people move through, the expectations placed on them, the policies guiding them, and the communities they belong to.

As a well-being leader, your role is to "shovel the ramp," so to speak—removing barriers, smoothing the path, and ensuring equitable access for everyone. This means not only creating supportive conditions but also equipping individuals with empowering life skills to advocate for themselves, manage their health, and participate as resilient, contributing members of their communities.

If we fully realize this vision, the need for dedicated well-being roles would decrease, because thriving would no longer require intervention; it would be woven into the fabric of organizational life. Here we can use another nature-inspired metaphor: the interconnected root systems of trees. Linked by underground fungi, trees share nutrients, send signals, and adapt as a community. On the surface, they may seem to stand alone, but in reality, they survive and flourish together. Similarly, people thrive when supported by the invisible networks of care and connection that surround them.

The HOW Constructs in Practice

The HOW ring is grounded in this two-prong approach to create meaningful change: nurturing individuals with skills and needed interpersonal supports, while also fostering a culture of care through systems, environments, and policies that make thriving the easy choice.

The following sections walk through each SEM level, bringing them to life. The first two are about nurturing individual care. The last three are about creating a culture of care.

Personal

The personal level emphasizes individual skills, attitudes, knowledge, and behaviors. It's where many wellness programs begin—yoga classes, healthy eating, and mindfulness. These are vital, but they aren't sufficient. Too often, people hear "You need to change" without considering the systems that enable sustainable transformation.

This approach is modeled on theories like Maslow's Hierarchy of Needs, Prochaska's Stages of Change, and the health belief model. As a leader, you recognize that personal responsibility is only part of the bigger picture. You're likely in your role because someone identified the need for a better approach, even if they weren't exactly sure what it should look like.

As I've mentioned, our industry today is moving toward more salutogenic strategies that focus on strengths and thriving, rather than merely fixing problems. Here people are no longer just objects of intervention but active partners in shaping their own well-being. Interdisciplinary, data-informed, and human-centered design remains vital.

Interpersonal

The interpersonal level recognizes that behavior change doesn't happen alone; it occurs within a community. Whether through social media or personal connections, peer support is crucial. Positive peer pressure fosters change.

For example, an employee wanted to become more active, so she started a lunchtime walking club. At first, only a handful joined, but as colleagues saw their peers walking together, more people began to join in, not wanting to miss out on the camaraderie. What started as an individual interest soon became a shared ritual of care, where the motivation came less from activity and more from belonging, while supporting healthy behaviors.

Organizational

This is where we weave well-being into systems, services, and culture. Too often, the focus is solely on programming. But real impact happens when you align strategies with institutional priorities, collaborate across departments, and gain leadership support.

The American Medical Association's road map for CWOs stresses systemic change and the removal of the "pebbles in the shoe"—those small ongoing frustrations that drain people.[39] Whether it's confusing mental health access points or unclear parking policies, these issues are important.

At one university, we observed students being double-booked for mental health counseling because they made appointments across multiple departments, unsure where to turn. They scheduled sessions with counseling, psychiatry, and/or wellness, simply looking for someone to talk to. They didn't care about the entry point or which department provided the service; they just needed help. To address this, we developed and promoted a unified One Mental Health access point. Whether in person or online, students could visit a single location to request assistance, and they would be directed to the appropriate service for their needs. This streamlined approach not only enhanced the student experience and removed an annoying "pebble," it also improved collaboration among departments, ensuring timely access and optimal support.

Environmental

The environment includes physical, digital, and psychological spaces. It's where people live, work, learn, shop, travel, and connect. It influences how they feel and what they do. A well-designed environment shows that people matter. Accommodations include green spaces, lactation rooms, safe sidewalks, and access to healthy food. It's about making the healthy choice the easy choice.

It's also about fairness. Social factors—including education, job opportunities, justice systems, recreation, housing, and income—have a greater impact on health than genetics or access to healthcare. Real life is complex. Staying active is difficult without safe sidewalks, and eating well is hard without access to healthy food.

According to the County Health Rankings Model (2014, Figure 4.1), health outcomes are shaped by a combination of behaviors and clinical care, which together account for roughly half of the influencing health factors. The remaining influence stems from social, economic, and physical environmental factors, underscoring the broader drivers of population health that extend beyond medical interventions. That's why addressing upstream and social determinants is essential. Ultimately, well-being professionals need to clean up the proverbial "pond" where they can support well-being.

A note on context: Environments and priorities differ significantly across communities—particularly in underserved areas or regions impacted by conflict or crisis—where safety and basic needs are the primary focus. In these settings, environmental work begins with protection and dignity, encompassing secure shelter and water; reliable information and digital access; safe and inclusive spaces to learn, work, and access services; and policies that reduce harm and discrimination.

As with all communities, but particularly here, progress should be…

- Participatory (designed with, not for, the community)
- Trauma-informed (reducing re-harm)

- Feasible (appropriate to local resources and infrastructure)
- Equity-oriented (focusing on those most affected)

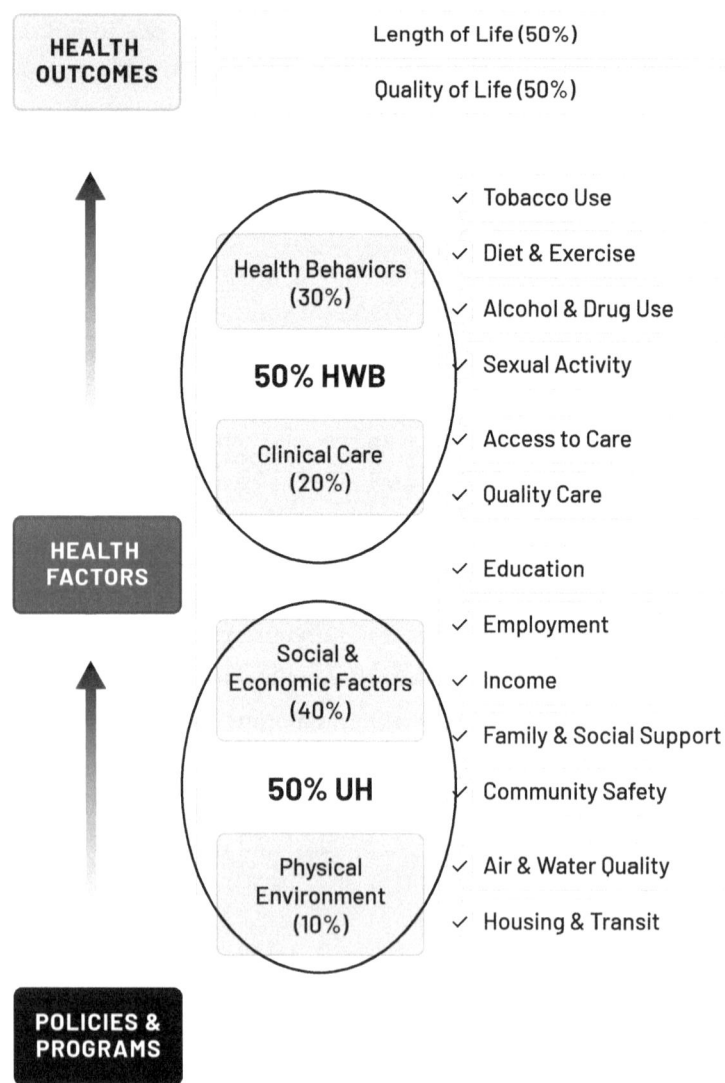

Figure 4.1: County Health Ranking Model[40]

The goal remains the same everywhere—to create conditions where people can belong and thrive—even if initial efforts focus on stability and safety before expanding to broader well-being services.

Policy

Sometimes change requires policies—whether it's big P ones like tobacco bans or small p ones like flexible work schedules. Well-designed policies establish social norms and support fairer structures.

The challenge is that systems often resist change, whether intentional or not. People may say they want change, but struggle to follow through. That's why policy remains vital for sustaining progress. When individuals face difficulties, the system offers support. Just as a strong culture helps someone navigate mental health challenges, a healthy person strengthens that culture in return.

History offers clear examples. In the 1980s, traffic fatalities were high. Public health had tried education and even engineered cars that put the seat belt on for us. But it wasn't until the Click It or Ticket campaign and policy took effect that behavior changed.[41] The same was true with tobacco—awareness and education weren't enough, but tobacco-free policies drove lasting behavior change. Today, both seat belt use and tobacco-free environments are the norm, largely because policies reinforced the changes that people struggled to sustain on their own and health improved.

Just like all the other rings in the Harrington Well-Being Model, there is no one-size-fits-all approach to the HOW. Success comes from synergy across multiple levels: individual and interpersonal support, organizational systems, environmental design, and policies that promote a culture of well-being. When these elements align, they form a cohesive strategy capable of driving change. Together, they create a unified approach for a collective impact.

So What's Your HOW Today?

The HOW is a strategic, multi-level approach that brings well-being to life and integrates it across individual, interpersonal, organizational, environmental, and policy levels. Based on the Socio-Ecological Model, this approach moves us beyond simply changing individual behavior to transforming the systems, environments, and cultures that shape well-being. While yoga classes and wellness programs are visible and helpful, they are not enough—we also need to design systems that promote care, equity, and a sense of belonging.

Your challenge is to align operations with purpose, shifting from *doing* healthy to truly *being* healthy. Whether redesigning access points or cleaning the proverbial "pond," the HOW is about weaving care into the design of spaces, policies, and daily practices—so that well-being becomes not just a goal but a core part of organizational life.

Make It Yours! Make It Happen!

Your HOW is the bridge between ideas and action. It's about delivering well-being strategies at multiple levels—individual, interpersonal, organizational, environmental, and policy—to make lasting change. The same approach can be adapted across these levels for a bigger, more enduring impact.

Clarify Your Pathways

1. **Map your reach.** Which socio-ecological levels (individual, interpersonal, organizational, environmental, policy) are you currently addressing?

2. **Spot the gaps.** Which levels are missing? How could you adapt an existing strategy to fill one of them?

3. **Think scale.** What is one action you could take this month to make your strategy more sustainable or scalable?

CHAPTER 5

Practices to Include the Upstream WHEN

H ave you noticed how many programs and services are reactive, centered on intervention and fixing problems after they occur? That was my world in healthcare: caring for sick people. Over time, I realized I didn't want my work to focus only on their illness; I wanted to help keep people from getting sick in the first place. That realization drew me into prevention. And it wasn't long before my vision expanded even further, beyond "not sick" to imagining people and communities truly thriving and flourishing.

One of my favorite well-being parables is about two people fishing in a river. They're enjoying the day when suddenly someone floats downstream, struggling in the water. The couple jumps in, rescues them, and goes back to fishing. Soon another person appears. And then another. Eventually, one of them heads upstream to find out why people are falling in. They discover that people are falling off the cliff into the water, so they build a fence. As has often been attributed to Archbishop Desmond Tutu: "There comes a point where we need to stop just pulling people out of the river. We need to go upstream and find out why they're falling in."

This story reflects a culture of quality and an upstream systems mindset, like tobacco and seat belts: Identify root causes, fix the system, and prevent harm from happening in the first place. As we've broadened our understanding of well-being to include emotional, social, spiritual, and professional aspects, we've also updated our strategies. One of the most impactful changes has been adopting this public health "upstream" approach—focusing on root causes rather than only addressing them through "downstream" treatment.

> Think upstream; act holistically.
> When you plan across the whole spectrum, you shift from reacting to reimagining—building systems that prevent harm, restore health, and promote thriving.

Wondering why the upstream approach matters so much? According to the 80/20 rule, we often spend 80% of our resources helping the 20% who have already fallen into crisis, whether it involves managing chronic illness, burnout, or financial stress. These downstream services are essential but costly, both financially and emotionally.

Conversely, investing in upstream prevention and promotion is more cost-effective and has a greater impact. It enables more people to thrive—not just survive—by addressing conditions before they become crises, similar to shoveling the ramp.

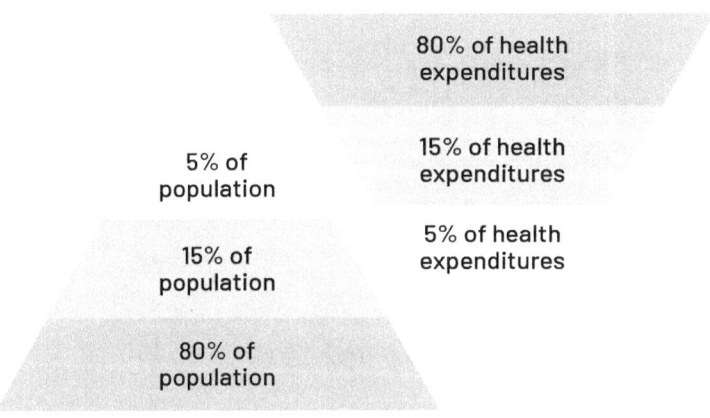

Figure 5.1: Population and Health Expenditures

The upstream approach is particularly important for tackling health disparities. It looks at societal-level factors—such as housing, transportation, education, income, and systemic discrimination—that influence daily life and long-term opportunities. These factors not only influence individual choices but also establish the boundaries and possibilities for those choices. For marginalized populations, upstream thinking isn't just helpful, it's crucial. Only by addressing structural inequities can we establish conditions that promote health and well-being for everyone. And while some of this work may be beyond the scope of your organization, it is crucial to keep these dynamics in mind when considering WHO populations.

The Continuum of Care

Imagine the cliff and river parable as a way to visualize the continuum of care.

- **Intervention** is pulling people out of the water, or an ambulance.
- **Risk reduction** stretches a safety net partway down the cliff.
- **Prevention** builds a fence at the top.
- **Promotion** helps people and communities thrive, so they don't drift anywhere near the edge.
- Many organizations also add a fifth element—**recovery**—for those climbing back after a fall.

Although I had long championed upstream thinking, I hadn't explicitly included this full spectrum of care in the original Harrington Well-Being Model. As a result, professionals in counseling, healthcare, and disability services—whose work often falls into midstream or downstream—felt left out of the conversation as I emphasized promotion. Yet their roles are essential to any health-promoting organization. Recognizing this led to the creation of the WHEN ring. Health professionals have long recognized that treatment alone is insufficient. Over time, care models expanded to include education, prevention, and then promotion—embracing a salutogenic (health-creating) approach rather than only a pathogenic (disease-focused) one.

The truth is, it's not about choosing one approach over another. It is a big AND, integrating downstream, midstream, and upstream strategies across the full wellness–illness continuum.

TRADITIONAL APPROACH	AND	UPSTREAM APPROACH
Reactive		Proactive
Downstream		Upstream
Pathogenic		Salutogenic
Needs based		Strengths based
Risk reduction/intervention		Promotion/prevention
Programs and services		Systems and settings
Individual-focused		Community-focused
Traditions		Innovation

Figure 5.2: The Big AND

Let's explore each aspect of WHEN in relation to the continuum of care more closely.

Intervention (Tertiary Care): This is downstream reactive care such as medical treatment, counseling, and crisis response. It's essential but often costly and complex. I often compare it to an ambulance: It's there when needed but ideally not your only strategy. It's most effective when the person actively participates in their care.

Risk Reduction (Safety Nets): Midstream strategies catch people early, before situations worsen. These include chronic disease management, mental health support, accommodations, and early detection such as screenings. Many individuals operate in this space, navigating long-term conditions or managing ongoing challenges. They may be in recovery or restoration. The metaphor here is the safety net.

Prevention (Primary Prevention): Still midstream, primary prevention aims to stop problems before they begin. These include programs often associated with wellness such as nutrition education, stress management, and suicide prevention. This is the fence at the top of the cliff.

Promotion (Upstream): Promotion reaches even further upstream to cultivate a culture and environment where people can thrive. It involves proactive health-focused efforts that promote a sense of belonging, purpose, joy, and vitality. When you combine the imagery of the ambulance, the safety net, and the fence at the top of the cliff, promotion creates a world where fewer ambulances are needed, nets catch fewer falls, and people and communities can thrive and flourish safely at the top.

Here's an example of engaging all levels of the framework: When we lacked internal data on employee health, we started with national data, which unsurprisingly highlighted hypertension, diabetes, and cardiovascular disease as primary concerns. Addressing these required a mix of downstream, midstream, and upstream strategies.

- On the downstream side, we expanded access to medical care and counseling by bringing in nurse practitioners and offering screenings to identify employees at risk for prediabetes or prehypertension.

- Midstream strategies focused on prevention—encouraging movement, healthy nutrition, adequate sleep, and stress management—to reduce risk factors before they developed into chronic conditions.

- Upstream, we aimed to create environments that promoted thriving and flourishing for all, adding walking trails, healthier food options, and even a walking labyrinth to encourage both physical activity and mental restoration.

This same layered approach applies to burnout and mental health. Strong downstream services provide essential crisis care, while supportive upstream environments reduce stress and foster meaning, purpose, and connection—making it more likely that employees stay healthy, engaged, and resilient.

So What Is Your WHEN Today?

WHEN is pervasive; it's focused on aligning well-being strategies throughout the entire care spectrum—promotion, prevention, risk reduction, intervention, and recovery—allowing you to respond effectively to crises and also proactively create flourishing environments where people can thrive. While many organizations emphasize downstream services like counseling and medical care, true health-promoting systems incorporate upstream approaches that address root causes and social determinants such as housing, transportation, belonging, and purpose.

The WHEN ring reminds us that timing is critical: We need ambulances *and* fences, safety nets *and* flourishing gardens. By integrating strategies across all levels, we ensure that well-being becomes a coordinated, inclusive, and sustainable part of daily life for everyone.

Make It Yours! Make It Happen!

Your WHEN covers the entire spectrum of care—from prevention to early intervention and recovery. Too often, well-being efforts focus solely on one aspect of the journey. A well-rounded approach ensures your organization supports individuals at every stage.

Define Your Practices

1. **Check your balance.** Which parts of the continuum (promotion, prevention, risk reduction, treatment) receive the most attention and resources?

2. **Close the gaps.** Where could you expand or connect efforts to better support people across the full spectrum—promotion through treatment?

3. **Adapt to change.** How is your organization evolving its strategies to meet the shifting needs, trends, and expectations in well-being?

SECTION TWO

ACTIVATING YOUR HARRINGTON WELL-BEING MODEL

Now that you've explored the complexities of health-promoting organizations, it's time to activate the rings by tailoring them to your specific context, role, and organization. In this section, you'll examine each ring in detail and identify ways to adapt it to your setting. Additionally, you'll take a closer look at the interconnectedness of the rings, guided by real-world examples from my work at the University of Houston.

One note about the *Make It Yours! Make It Happen!* exercises in this section: They're designed to help you start crafting your own version of the model—one that aligns with your organization's purpose, language, and culture. That way, the next time you ask your leader what to prioritize and they say, "All of it," you'll be able to nod and smile, because you have a game plan to navigate the complexity and intersectionality of your job.

As you build your own model, I'll use a version from the University of Houston as a demonstration. This and other model illustrations are also available on www.SuzyHarrington.com under Model.

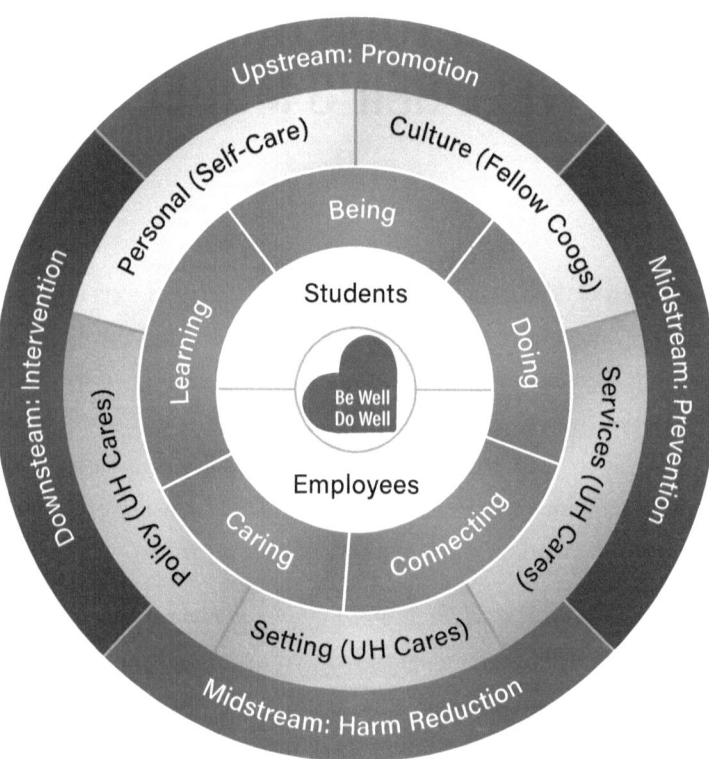

Figure Section 2.1: University of Houston Adaptation of the Harrington Well-Being Model, 2025

Practices to Include the Upstream WHEN

Use this model template and make it your own—filling it in and adapting it as you work through the rings in the upcoming chapters of this section.

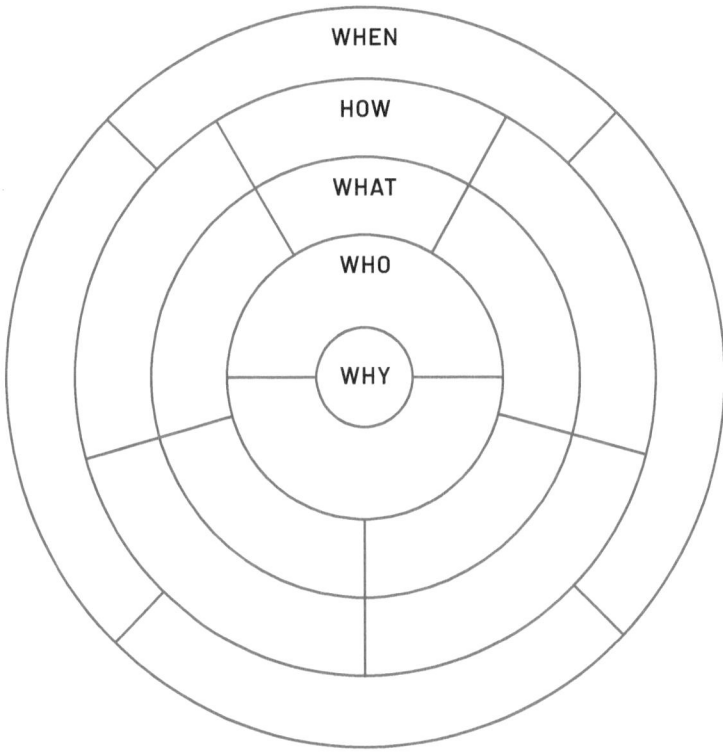

Figure Section 2.2: Harrington Well-Being Model Template

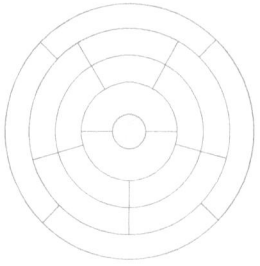

CHAPTER 6

Anchoring Your Purpose (WHY)

When I first took on a wellness leadership role, I felt the weight of the entire system on my shoulders. Each department had its own priorities, and every team spoke its own language. There were impressive "pockets of excellence," but no unifying framework to connect them. As a new CWO, I needed a way to connect the dots—to understand the landscape, communicate across silos, and most importantly, lead with clarity and strategy.

That's when the Harrington Well-Being Model began to take shape, with each ring representing a different priority perspective, which had increased the complexity and confusion. By organizing them into rotating rings, it became both a strategic and visual tool to transform scattered efforts into a unified, aligned, and sustainable approach—a way to turn theory into systems-level action.

As you learned in the first section, the WHY is the bullseye at the very center of the Harrington Well-Being Model because everything else revolves around it. Your values, priorities, strategies, and stakeholders all gain clarity and focus from this core. Without a shared purpose, well-being efforts can become fragmented, siloed, or reactive. But when rooted in purpose, they become transformational.

It Begins with Your WHY

Whether you're developing an organizational well-being strategy, launching a program, leading a committee, or inspiring a movement, identifying your mission or shared purpose is the essential first step. This is true not only for organizations but also for you personally. While a WHY might eventually be expressed in a slogan or image, it begins with honest reflection, careful listening, and thoughtful collaboration. This is true across all settings—campuses, hospitals, neighborhoods, places of worship, businesses, salons, and correctional institutions alike.

When asked about my leadership style, I used to say, "Servant leadership with open communication." But over time, I've realized my core approach is "purpose-driven leadership"—linking everyday actions to a greater purpose, creating a sense of meaning, and aligning short-term wins with a long-term vision. I've often described this vision like the point of an arrow, aligning our collective focus along its shaft. In times of uncertainty or chaos, it offers direction.

One image that stayed with me comes from driver training: If you focus on the guardrails, you're more likely to hit them. But if you focus on where you want to go, you're more likely to get there. Your WHY keeps your eyes on the road ahead.

> Your WHY is both an anchor and an invitation. Let it evolve as you grow and allow it to guide you with courage and compassion.

A powerful purpose doesn't develop in isolation—it emerges within community. As one colleague said, "There is no community without unity." A clear shared WHY helps reduce duplication, boost collaboration, and enhance teamwork across departments. That's one reason many organizations feel siloed: They haven't taken the time to define what well-being truly means for them or how they will work toward it together.

I once heard of an East Coast hospital where every employee, from the CEO to the janitor, could explain how their role contributed to patient care. Similar to the concept of Health in All Policies,[42] that deeply resonated with me and continues to influence how I think about well-being in all roles and at all levels.

We're witnessing a remarkable shift—from wellness to well-being; from individual programs to systems thinking; from physical health to the full spectrum of social, spiritual, emotional, and professional flourishing. This evolution, however, adds complexity. Many well-meaning leaders are doing valuable work but it is too often in silos or without strategic alignment. Imagine all those efforts moving in the same direction, like the one big arrow. That's the power of collective impact. The Harrington Well-Being Model integrates all five into its very design.

Finding and Aligning Your WHY

Begin by examining your organization's existing mission, vision, and values. What language is already in use? Which goals are already emphasized? Your well-being WHY should support the larger purpose, even if it isn't identical. For example, in a hospital, the mission might be to heal patients, but the well-being strategy could focus on nurturing the health and resilience of the team doing that work.

Engage leadership early to understand their expectations. Hold listening sessions or meet and greets with teams, students, employees, or community members. Ask questions like these:

- What does well-being mean to you?
- What does success look like?
- What feels like support—and what feels like a barrier?

Over time, patterns will emerge that clarify your WHY and components within the other rings—what is prioritized and what may be overlooked.

Use these conversations to gently shift outdated mindsets. Reframe well-being as essential to performance, retention, creativity, student success, and community connection—not an extra, but a multiplier. Pay attention to the language used by HR, advancement, academic affairs, finance, or operations, and speak it. Translate your purpose into terms they value: ROI, VOI, belonging, retention, or culture.

Purpose can surprise you. At one elite university, the unspoken goal for students was to graduate with a six-figure job. But I heard from several students who found their WHY in the outdoor adventure program. There they learned to lead, to camp, to climb… and to belong. Similarly, I found my purpose not in my nursing coursework but in ROTC (Reserve Officers' Training Corps), where I learned discipline, camaraderie, and leadership. Yes—I'm ROTC and proud!

Dr. Victor Strecher, a leader in digital health and behavior change, describes purpose as a "miracle drug," one that extends life, improves outcomes, and increases motivation. In his book *Life on Purpose*, he views purpose as both a form of prevention and a source of connection. He reminds us that meaning isn't a luxury; it's a vital sign.[43]

While in higher education, my own "aha" moment occurred in 2014, while reading Gallup's *Great Jobs, Great Lives* report.[44] For years, higher education has focused on student well-being. But the goal wasn't just successful students—it was thriving graduates. That small shift helped me reframe our work: from the classroom to the commencement stage and into the lives, families, and communities our students would eventually impact. A sports analogy that helps hockey players succeed is to think about where the puck is going, rather than where it currently is. In the same way, our goal wasn't just about where students were in the moment, but about where they were headed—their success as thriving graduates and lifelong global citizens.

Language Shapes Culture

As you begin to write your WHY, choose words that energize possibility. Consider phrases like "flourishing communities" or "living our best selves"—language that focuses on what people can become, not just what they need to overcome. Following are some sample vision or purpose statements that have emerged from my work.

- "Living our best selves personally and professionally within the communities where we live, learn, work, and play so that we can make a difference for ourselves, our families, and our community."

- "We cultivate a community of care to promote and enrich the health and well-being of our students so that they can become successful scholars and engaged global citizens."

- "Being, doing, connecting, caring, and learning—together."

Your slogan or trademark can evolve, and many organizations start there. Past examples include the following:

- "America's Healthiest Campus" (Oklahoma State University, 2014)
- "Smart and Happy" (Georgia Tech student-led proposal, 2017)
- "Be Your Best You" (Texas Children's, 2022)
- "Be Well to Do Well" (University of Houston, 2025)

Let's examine that last example more closely. The University of Houston focused on highlighting the link between well-being and academic achievement. Their WHY meets the criterion of being unique to the organization, helping to inspire others with a clear sense of purpose and direction.

Figure 6.1: *University of Houston WHY Bullseye Example: Your Purpose*

At the heart is the why—the purpose that aligns with the institution's mission and values. At the University of Houston, this is expressed as "Be Well to Do Well," highlighting the connection between well-being and academic success. The WHY must be unique to the organization to begin inspiring others around the true purpose and your destination.

Remember, your WHY is more than a statement—it's your anchor, your compass, and your invitation. It centers you when things get messy, motivates you when energy wanes, and connects others to something greater than themselves. Whether you're launching a new initiative or realigning an existing one, this chapter is your opportunity to pause, reflect, and articulate the purpose that will guide your path. Don't worry about getting it perfect; just make it honest. The rest of the work will become clearer as you lead with clarity, engage others confidently, and build a culture where well-being isn't just a program but also a shared way of being.

If you're struggling to define it, start with what already exists—then listen, ask, reflect, and refine. Let your WHY be aspirational and actionable. A strong WHY helps prioritize audiences (WHO), select wellness dimensions (WHAT), choose impactful strategies (HOW), and focus your efforts across the continuum (WHEN).

From this bullseye, everything else can begin to align.

Make It Yours! Make It Happen!

Your purpose is the anchor that keeps your efforts grounded, your team aligned, and your culture evolving clearly. It's more than a mission; it's the heartbeat of your strategy. Whether inherited, newly discovered, or co-created with your community, your WHY should inspire, unite, and last. Define it with courage, revisit it intentionally, and let it become the force that turns effort into meaning.

Step One: Reflect on Your WHY

Use these prompts to explore the origins of your personal well-being purpose and how it aligns with your organization's mission and well-being purpose.

- **Origins:** Where did your beliefs about well-being originate—professional training, personal experiences, or cultural influences?
- **Motivation:** What drives your personal and professional dedication to this work? What is your WHY?
- **Vision of Success:** What does individual *thriving* and community *flourishing* look like in your organization? If well-being were prioritized, what would people say about working, learning, and living here?

- **Current Organizational WHY:** How would you describe your organization's current purpose or main focus related to well-being—such as prevention, performance, equity, engagement, or another area?

- **Language Alignment:** What existing language already connects to well-being in your organization's mission, values, recruiting materials, or leadership messages? If none exists, what language could you introduce to make that connection?

- **Program Purpose Check:** Are your current programs and initiatives clearly connected to a deeper purpose?

- **Disconnects:** Where do you see a gap between WHAT is being done and WHY it's being done?

Step Two: Draft a Statement of Purpose

Use this framework to draft a single, compelling sentence or tagline that articulates the aspirational purpose of your organization's well-being efforts and can serve as a starting point for conversations, setting the bullseye for your model. Try using the template below.

> "We foster [what kind of environment or culture] so that [our people] can [do or become] in [your context or community]."

For inspiration, review the sample vision and purpose statements shared earlier in this chapter. Try to make it clear enough to guide decisions, inspiring enough to motivate action, and aligned with your organization's core mission and values.

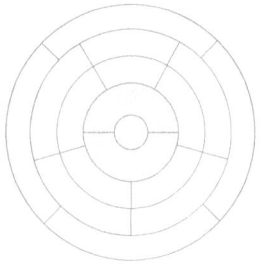

CHAPTER 7

Understanding Your People and Their Needs (WHO)

The WHO ring intentionally sits next to the WHY in the Harrington Well-Being Model because people are the heartbeat of any organization. You must start with the understanding that every person—regardless of their role or identity—deserves dignity, belonging, and the freedom to be seen as more than a label. A whole-person approach values each individual's experiences and contributions. Your purpose guides your population's needs, but the people within your WHO ring shape your strategies, programs, and priorities.

Before selecting a program or topic, consider who you are serving. This includes everyone within the organizational ecosystem—for example, students, faculty, staff, employees, volunteers, and community members—each with their own lived experience, identity, and needs. A health-promoting organization not only recognizes this diversity but also actively designs for it. This means moving beyond assumptions to create structures where all people feel seen, valued, and supported. Designing for inclusion involves ensuring that justice, access, and care are not just ideals but also integral parts of how you build systems and spaces for well-being.

You don't design for the average; you design for all. That includes physical safety, emotional safety, meaningful connection, and clear pathways to navigate one's environment. It also means providing the tools, training, time, and trust needed to do your job or pursue your studies effectively. When well-being is prioritized with people at the center, outcomes improve across the board: relevance, participation, trust, and impact.

Recognizing this complexity isn't just about identity—it's about access. It's about ensuring that programming, communication, resources, and systems are designed to reflect, respect, and respond to the people they intend to serve, and making sure you are reaching the right people to achieve your aspirational WHY.

Obstacles You Might Face in Designing for Inclusivity

Even in organizations with strong leadership and passionate frontline teams, well-being efforts often stall, especially at the middle management level, because they typically face many conflicting priorities. These leaders are often caught between competing demands, managing operational tasks without clear guidance or the ability to prioritize well-being. Too often, well-being is viewed as a "nice to have" rather than a strategic priority. That's why the WHO matters so much. Without a clear understanding of the people you serve—and those leading and supporting these services—your efforts may be well-intentioned but misaligned.

Focusing on the WHO reminds you that everyone in an organization is part of the community. No matter their title, background, or role, people share essential needs. Everyone wants to feel safe—physically, emotionally, and culturally. They want to feel seen, valued, and heard. They also long to feel connected, to belong, and to contribute in a meaningful way. And they need nourishment, movement, rest, and spaces to restore themselves. These aren't optional—they are fundamental.

Designing for the WHO goes beyond demographics or segmentation. It's about respecting dignity. It's about looking past roles and labels to understand the lived experiences, identities, and needs that influence each person's ability to thrive. And it's about actively removing barriers—whether physical, systemic, cultural, or attitudinal—to ensure full participation and well-being.

When you get the WHO right, everything changes. You build credibility into the foundation of your efforts. You design for relevance and access. Engagement increases—not because you mandated participation, but because people feel invited, included, and supported. And perhaps most importantly, when you align your audiences with your organizational purpose, you stop spinning in silos and start building unified momentum. Because when people feel well, they engage well, lead well, learn well, work well, and live well. And that's the heart of a health-promoting organization.

> To serve effectively, you must see clearly. Value both the familiar and the overlooked, because everyone deserves to be part of the picture.

Every organization contains smaller subgroups with unique experiences and needs. Understanding these differences helps you avoid one-size-fits-all solutions. Ask yourself:

What groups naturally exist within my organization or community?

How do people self-identify or differentiate by location, job type, lived experience, or stage of life?

In higher education, audiences are often grouped into students, faculty, and staff—but within these categories are meaningful subpopulations, including first-generation students, international students, commuters versus residents, graduate assistants, nontraditional learners, adjunct faculty, tenured faculty, and custodial staff. Faculty and staff may also be segmented by department, leadership role, contract status, or physical location. Some institutions also include alumni, extension offices, or satellite campuses, each with its unique dynamics.

In workplaces, segmentation can be even more nuanced. For example, in a hospital or large organization, you might consider job roles (such as physician, nurse, technician, food services), work location, shift times, employment status (full-time, part-time, contractor), education level, language, caregiving responsibilities, tenure, leadership level, and cultural identifiers such as race, gender, or faith. Don't forget volunteers, interns, hybrid employees, or remote workers—all are part of the organizational ecosystem and deserve to be included in your well-being lens.

In community settings, subgroups can be organized by age, income, language, geography, or shared interests and social identities. Faith communities, neighborhood groups, nonprofits, and civic organizations often serve as trusted connectors and key audiences. Recognizing these differences is essential for designing *with*, and not just *for*, the people you aim to serve.

Be thoughtful in how you define your groups. Limit to no more than five subgroup headers. Each header can include various descriptor words. Consider whether traditional divisions, like separating students and employees for funding, still serve your well-being goals. Who might be overlooked? Are programs only available during business hours, even though your organization operates 24/7? These are not just logistical issues; they are design choices with implications for fairness. When you know your WHO, you can design intentionally—and with impact.

You as the Conductor of the Culture

Your role is to connect the dots—to listen, learn, and align. You are the conductor of the well-being orchestra. Each department, role, or subgroup is like a different section: strings, percussion, woodwinds. Each has its rhythms, priorities, and tone. Each is important. And when you work from a shared vision, framework, and purpose, everyone's reading the same sheet of music. Together, you're creating something that resonates.

Use your meet and greets, listening sessions, and needs assessments to identify your stakeholders, allies, and early adopters. Apply concepts from Everett Rogers' Diffusion of Innovation Theory, which describes how new ideas and practices spread through a population.[45] Map your stakeholders to understand who your innovators, early adopters, majority groups, and laggards are. Understand their language, motivators, and challenges.

Who already sees well-being as central?

Who are the influencers?

Who is absent from the conversation?

And who might slow progress if not engaged?

- **Innovators** (about 2.5%) are risk-takers and experimenters who enjoy trying new things first. They're often your champions for pilot projects.

- **Early Adopters** (about 13.5%) are respected opinion leaders who quickly recognize the benefits and can influence others. Their support helps build momentum.

- **Early Majority** (about 34%) are more deliberate; they adopt after seeing proven results and trusted peers on board.

- **Late Majority** (about 34%) tend to be skeptical and adopt only after most others have done so.

- **Laggards** (about 16%) resist change the longest, often because of tradition, mistrust, or resource constraints.

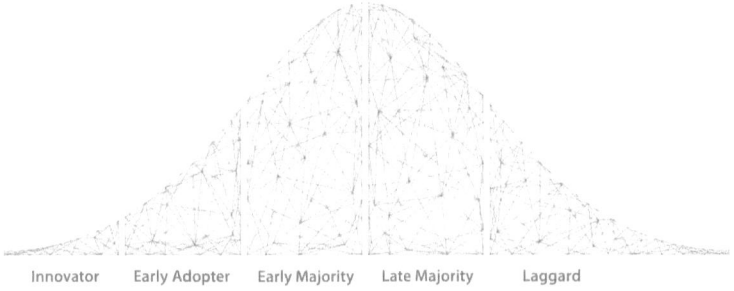

Innovator   Early Adopter   Early Majority   Late Majority   Laggard

Figure 7.1: Diffusion of Innovation Model

Also recognize that many people belong to multiple groups. For example, a graduate student might also be a full-time employee, caregiver, or first-generation college student. People's experiences are layered. That's why intersectionality is essential when identifying your WHO. Be especially mindful of those often overlooked: night-shift workers, remote employees, non-native English speakers, or members of historically marginalized communities.

Consider your organizational purpose. If your primary mission is serving patients, students, or clients, ask yourself: Are they the direct recipients of our well-being efforts, or do they benefit indirectly from a thriving culture?

In many healthcare settings, for example, patients are not the WHO of internal well-being strategies—employees are. In this case, you would choose not to focus on the patients directly, as you know that a thriving staff culture leads to better outcomes for everyone. The parts of the WHO should support your WHY.

By clearly defining who you serve—your primary and priority groups—you'll be better prepared to develop strategies (the WHAT), environments and systems (the HOW), and timing (the

WHEN) that align with your purpose (the WHY). Here's an at-a-glance look at how each ring intersects with WHO.

- **WHO ↔ WHY** Different audiences might have different reasons for engaging.

- **WHO ↔ WHAT** Needs differ by group; don't assume one size fits all.

- **WHO ↔ HOW** Some groups require more systems support; others succeed with peer-to-peer models.

- **WHO ↔ WHEN** Readiness, vulnerability, and equity require different timing. Identify needs and meet them, but focus on helping people flourish, which involves addressing both downstream and upstream needs, prioritizing the latter.

Public health, diversity work, and workplace well-being all offer valuable tools for segmenting populations and providing support. But the real magic happens when you combine that data with empathy and partnership. When you truly understand who you serve—and design accordingly—you transition from superficial wellness to transformative well-being.

For example, at the University of Houston, first-year students were identified as a group (WHO) that needed stronger emotional and academic support (WHAT). To match their needs, upstream strategies were introduced during orientation (WHEN), and peer mentoring (HOW) was used to reinforce early belonging.

Understanding Your People and Their Needs (WHO)

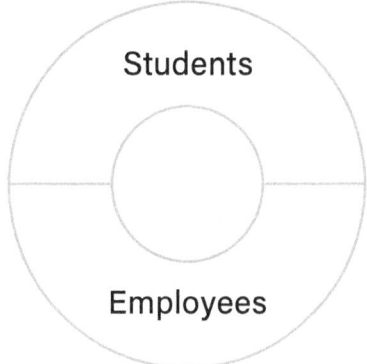

Figure 7.2: UH WHO Ring Example: Your Target Audience

The WHO represent audiences served: students, faculty, staff, and often the broader community. Clarity here ensures inclusive and effective strategy design.

Make It Yours! Make It Happen!

Your people are the reason your work exists, and the greatest asset in bringing your vision to life. Designing for inclusion means recognizing the full humanity in each role, title, and story. Whether you serve a few or many, what matters most is that every person feels seen, supported, and connected. Listen deeply, design boldly, and let your WHO become the heartbeat of your culture of care.

Step One: Reflection

Before you can effectively engage people in your well-being strategy, you need to be clear about WHO you are serving and *who* can help you make it happen. Use these questions to guide your thinking.

- Which subgroups could play a key role in implementing your WHY?

- Who are the most visible audiences in your organization? Who are the least visible or often overlooked?

- Which groups are essential to the culture but may not be represented in decision-making?

- What's one group you could listen to more intentionally before launching your next initiative?

- Are there groups that wield influence both informally and formally? (Think beyond job titles—consider student leaders, respected peers, or community champions.)

Step Two: Make It Official

1. Using your answers from Step One, identify up to **five main subgroups** to place in your WHO ring.

2. Then break each subgroup into smaller specific segments using descriptive words. This helps you see differences within groups and tailor strategies accordingly.

Create a simple two-column table similar to the following example.

YOUR PEOPLE CATEGORIES	DESCRIPTOR WORDS
University Employees	faculty, staff, student staff, volunteers
University Students	undergraduate, transfer, graduate, professional, residents
Community Partners	local nonprofits, health agencies, faith-based groups
Alumni & Supporters	recent graduates, long-term alumni, donors, advocates

Table 7.1: *People Categories Example – Your WHO*

This exercise not only clarifies your audience but also serves as a reference point for program planning, communications, and evaluation. Over time as your organization evolves, you can revisit and revise your chart.

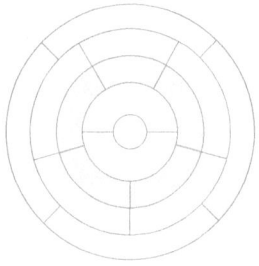

CHAPTER 8

Prioritizing Your Wellness Dimensions (WHAT)

Activating the WHAT in this model involves addressing the essential dimensions of well-being—physical, emotional, social, spiritual, and professional—that help individuals and organizations flourish. These dimensions are not isolated; they are interconnected and shaped by personal experiences and environmental factors.

An example of this is when a new nurse told me she almost quit during her first six months. What kept her going was a preceptor who not only taught her clinical skills but also checked in about how she was doing outside of work. That relationship encompassed every dimension:

- Physical, through modeling practices such as safe patient handling
- Emotional, by fostering trust and reducing stress
- Social, by giving her a sense of belonging
- Spiritual, by connecting her to the deeper purpose of caring for families
- Professional, by shaping her career development

She told me later, "It wasn't the training manual that kept me here—it was her."

Ultimately, the words you include within these dimensions are more than just a model—they convey a message. They reveal what your organization values and how you prioritize caring for your people. When thoughtfully identified and defined, and clearly communicated, they serve as both a mirror and a guide: reflecting the current state of well-being within your population and steering you toward your shared vision of flourishing. Through shared language, connected insights, and inclusive dialogue, your WHAT becomes a unifying force—grounded in evidence, driven by purpose, and shaped by the people it serves.

> What you name, you nurture. Choose words and ideas that resonate, reflect, and connect with people where they are.

Crucially, language influences both perception and behavior. That's why the WHAT ring is often the most debated. People express strong opinions based on their training, profession, or personal priorities. The words you choose can unite or inspire…or unintentionally exclude. That's why buy-in is important, and so is clarity. When identifying dimensions, it's crucial to agree on their meanings and the descriptors used to define them. Do your terms match your culture and population?

Choose upstream, salutogenic, asset-based terms. For example, "thriving" is more aspirational than "avoiding burnout." "Nutrition" encourages lifestyle change more than "diet," which can imply restriction or shame. Even if some people need targeted interventions like diet plans or exercise prescriptions, your organizational language should focus on long-term flourishing, not temporary fixes.

Also, consider organizational culture. In one federal agency, we were unable to use Spiritual as a dimension, despite having defined it broadly (purpose, joy, awe). The religious connotation was too strong. So we adapted. Being responsive is part of inclusive design.

Thinking Beyond the Standard

Sometimes well-being professionals default to what's familiar. In higher education, the main wellness priorities are often mental health, substance misuse, and sexual violence prevention. These are vital topics, but they don't represent the entire picture.

As I mentioned in Chapter 3, one of my early teams struggled with traditional wellness categories. We pivoted toward action-oriented words—doing, caring, connecting, learning, and being—which became much more engaging and relatable.

New frameworks may emerge from national leaders or internal departments, and they might initially seem to conflict. Don't panic. Crosswalking these frameworks can reveal alignment and build trust.

What is a crosswalk? It's a simple visual tool, often a table, that maps out connections between models, helping translate one set of concepts into another. It bridges language and fosters integration.

For example, when I returned to the University of Houston in an interim role, their model had already identified their well-being dimensions. Around that time, the U.S. Surgeon General released the *Workplace Mental Health & Well-Being*.[46] A few months later, Paul Wesselmann (widely known as "The Ripples Guy") led an afternoon workshop on well-being during the Division of Student Affairs all-staff retreat, introducing his four-part model.[47]

Were they at odds? No. A quick crosswalk showed that all three frameworks aligned with the current model. This alignment provided legitimacy, encouraged buy-in, and helped leaders see their priorities reflected in the larger picture.

Here's a visual representation of that crosswalk.

DIMENSION	UNIVERSITY OF HOUSTON	SURGEON GENERAL'S ESSENTIALS	PAUL "THE RIPPLES GUY" WE GOT THIS	HEALTH SYSTEM'S VALUES
Physical	Doing	Protection from harm	Nurture health	Mission of patient care
Emotional	Caring	Work-life harmony	Open hearts	Live compassionately
Spiritual	Being	Mattering at work	Calm spirits	Embrace freedom
Social	Connecting	Connection and community	Ripples action	Amplify unity
Professional	Learning	Opportunities for growth	Curious minds	Lead tirelessly

Table 8.1: Crosswalk Example

Walking through these connections, an assistant vice president (AVP) at the time had an "aha" moment and now uses the crosswalk in leadership discussions.

That's the power of visual alignment—it makes wellness click, just like the Harrington Well-Being Model!

This crosswalk example demonstrates how you can align within your organization and illustrate how the Harrington Well-Being Model can integrate seamlessly with well-established, evidence-based frameworks—whether global initiatives like Blue Zone's "Power 9" lifestyle habits shared by the world's longest-living and healthiest people, or sector-specific wellness models—while still maintaining a cohesive, organization-wide strategy.

Defining Your Dimensions and Descriptors

There's no single "correct" list of well-being dimensions. Start with what matters most to your people. Use your WHY and WHO to guide your WHAT. And choose language that uplifts, resonates, and reflects the direction you want to go.

Following are five broad categories, along with common descriptor words that I added to inspire your creativity. Remember, these are flexible and not set in stone. Use what works for your organization. Adjust as needed. Most importantly, make it your own.

Physical / Doing

This is the most familiar dimension, often linked to physical health. It both supports and is supported by all other dimensions.

- **Descriptors:** activity, sleep, nutrition, hydration, rest, prevention, safety, security, clinical care, violence-free, tobacco/substance-free, time management, nature, art, ergonomics, screen time, leisure
- **Note:** Leisure is essential recovery, not laziness. Take time to breathe, both literally and figuratively. Just as we inhale to inspire, we must exhale to let go.

Emotional / Caring

Often linked to mental health, this area includes emotional intelligence, regulation, and support systems that protect against stress and burnout.

- **Descriptors:** resilience, self-compassion, stress management skills, mental health, emotional intelligence, empathy, respect, flexibility, psychological safety, autonomy
- **Challenge:** Are we merely reacting to crises or actively building emotional health upstream and culturally?

Spiritual / Being

This goes beyond religion. It's about meaning, connection, and values alignment, both personally and collectively.

- **Descriptors:** purpose, joy, gratitude, awe, hope, fulfillment, mindfulness, transcendence, faith, optimism, service, dignity, and curiosity

- **Insight:** Mindfulness is more than meditation; being mindful of where you put your keys or whether you turned off the coffeepot can reduce your stress.

Social / Connecting

Belonging isn't just a bonus; it's a fundamental need. People thrive when they feel seen, safe, and supported.

- **Descriptors:** belonging, kindness, positive peer influence, inclusion, engagement, relationships, encouragement, shared identity
- **Observation:** COVID revealed how vital and fragile our social networks are.

Professional / Learning

This dimension includes personal and professional growth, creativity, financial wellness, and the pursuit of lifelong learning.

- **Descriptors:** learning, strengths, leadership, curiosity, digital literacy, academic success, creativity, failing forward, financial literacy, research
- **Reminder:** This is about more than just careers; it's how people manage their lives with purpose and confidence.

The Whole Ring

If one aspect is overlooked, everything can be affected. They are interconnected—more about harmony than perfect balance. And while your wellness wheel might show them as separate slices, your strategy should weave them all together.

Descriptor words play a powerful role in establishing that connection. In one university model, the front of the wheel displayed the dimensions, while the back featured carefully selected descriptor words. These words proved crucial: They shaped branding, messaging, and program development. (More on this in Chapter 13.) In fact, it was by using these descriptors and exploring intersections between them that leaders from different departments began to recognize their role in fostering cultural well-being.

Because the WHAT ring often becomes the visible wellness wheel and is frequently the entry point into your well-being strategy, the words you choose matter. They should resonate with your community, be marketable, and be prominently featured, such as on your website or in outreach materials.

When guiding the process of choosing dimensions, use participatory activities. Sticky notes, wall charts, and collaborative sorting can help people share ideas and agree on shared priorities. Then develop your language and reasoning together, while leaning into your expertise.

Prioritizing Your Wellness Dimensions (WHAT)

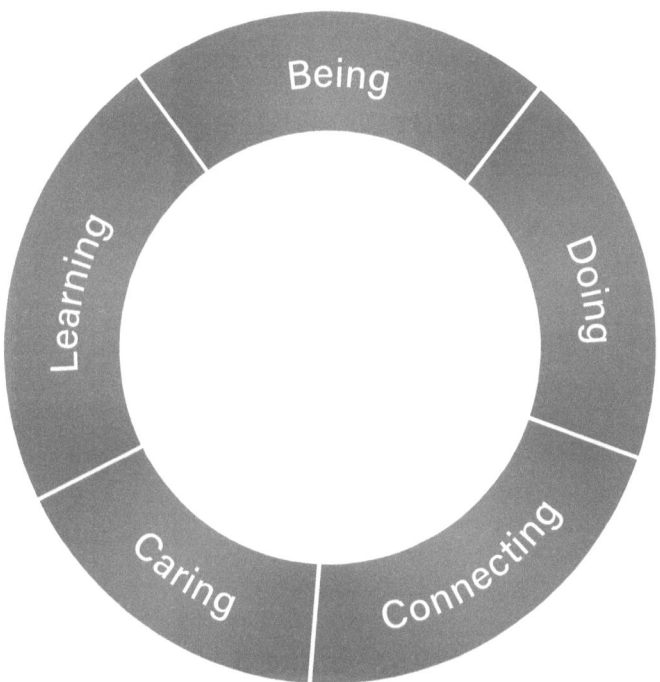

Figure 8.1: UH WHAT Ring Example: The Harmony of the Dimensions

The WHAT ring reflects the multidimensional nature of well-being; traditional wellness dimensions such as physical, emotional, social, and spiritual are expressed at UH through action-oriented games around being, doing, caring, connecting, and learning. Like the term and descriptor words, they should be customized to reflect the institution's unique culture, values, and language. Their adaptability enhances relevance, supports institution branding, and fosters a shared understanding and commitment to well-being.

Finally, keep these guiding questions in mind when considering how the WHAT ring intersects with the other rings.

- **WHAT ↔ WHY** Do your offerings reflect your shared values and mission?
- **WHAT ↔ WHO** Are your well-being dimensions aligned with your people?
- **WHAT ↔ HOW** Are the dimensions embedded across your systems?
- **WHAT ↔ WHEN** Are you addressing reactive needs or proactively promoting flourishing?

Make It Yours! Make It Happen!

The dimensions you choose and the words you use to describe them will influence how your people perceive themselves, interact with one another, and experience the culture of care within your organization. The right language can create connection, inspire engagement, and guide planning. Whatever you choose, ensure that it…

- Serves your purpose: aligns with your WHY
- Reflects your people: resonates with the lived experience and values of your WHO community
- Guides your planning: organizes strategies into clear, actionable areas

Choose confidently, refine collaboratively, and let your WHAT become the spark that connects hearts to strategy. Think of descriptor words as the front porch of your model—they're what people first see and feel. Make them engaging, accessible, and culturally relevant.

Step One: Reflection

Consider the following questions to guide your thinking.

1. Which dimensions or topics naturally resonate with your organization? Why?

2. What words or phrases are already in use (for example, in mission statements, values, recruitment materials) that could be integrated or adapted?

3. How might current or planned initiatives fit within one or more of these categories?

4. Are there dimensions that might be missing, or ones that could be reframed to be more inclusive or engaging?

Step Two: Draft Your Dimensions and Descriptor Words

Use the following table to begin defining your well-being dimensions.

1. In the first column, list the dimension or topic area (such as Physical, Social, Spiritual).

2. In the second column, identify descriptor words: action-oriented or emotionally resonant terms that capture the essence of that dimension for your organization.

WELL-BEING DIMENSION OR PRIORITIES	YOUR WORDS	YOUR DESCRIPTOR WORDS
Physical		
Emotional		
Spiritual		
Social		
Professional		

Table 8.2: Well-Being Dimensions – Your WHAT

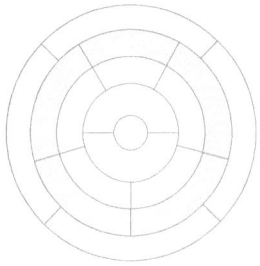

CHAPTER 9

Creating Pathways Across Your Levels of Influence (HOW)

When I was serving as the Air Force health promotion subject matter expert, a pediatrician approached me with a request: create a program to address the rising rates of childhood obesity. While well-intentioned, we recognized the flaw immediately: No child or parent wants to attend a program labeled "obesity." We knew we had the opportunity to effect bigger change and could not only market it but also design it more holistically. Instead of centering on obesity, we reframed the initiative around physical well-being and healthier communities. This shift in language removed stigma and opened doors for broader engagement.

We invited both children and parents to participate in a multi-week program that focused on activity, nutrition, and weight maintenance—without emphasizing weight loss. Together, we covered practical topics such as shopping, meal preparation, and enjoying snacks that are both healthy and enjoyable. Simple hands-on ideas like making Ants on a Log with celery, peanut butter, and raisins made nutrition approachable and memorable.

But we didn't stop there. Taking a broader socio-ecological approach, we expanded beyond the individual level. At the interpersonal level, families were encouraged to be active together—flying kites, walking the dog, or enjoying movement as play rather than exercise. At the organizational level, we partnered with the military childcare center to enhance food options. We collaborated with the fitness center to allow dependents to accompany their parents to the gym. These changes not only made healthy choices accessible but also integrated them into the culture and daily routines of military families.

The result was a program that reflected our purpose (health promotion), our audience (military families), and our method (interpersonal and institutional support). It was proactive, inclusive, and empowering. And it worked! Families, especially the children, were eager to share their stories—like reading food labels together and carving out time for walks—and in doing so, they modeled a culture of well-being that extended far beyond a single program.

We often concentrate our well-being efforts on the individual, teaching people what they need to do to be healthier. But behavior change doesn't occur in isolation. Imagine trying to eat healthier when every meeting in your office offers donuts or trying to walk more when your workplace lacks safe walking routes.

Even when people know what to do, social and cultural signals can override personal intentions. Seat belts are a classic example: Many resisted wearing them for years despite understanding their safety benefits. It wasn't until laws, social norms, and vehicle design aligned that people's behavior changed significantly.

That's why individual empowerment—teaching someone "to fish" rather than handing them the fish—must be combined with environments, systems, and cultures that make "fishing" possible, accessible, and rewarding. A truly health-promoting organization supports all: It equips individuals with the skills and confidence, while also ensuring the structures around them make thriving the easiest and most natural choice.

Culture isn't just about how things have always been done; it's about how you choose to do things going forward. Systems designed intentionally can either support outdated norms or foster true transformation. Your role is to align operations with purpose, moving from *doing* healthy to genuinely *being* healthy.

Sometimes that means clearing the path—shoveling ramps before stairs so everyone can enter. At other times, it's about redesigning workflows, policies, or spaces to encourage connection, rest, or physical movement. It could be as simple as offering flexible schedules to help prevent burnout…or as extensive as reimagining an entire onboarding process to focus on belonging and care.

Like the WHAT dimensions, there is no one-size-fits-all approach to the HOW. Effective strategies weave together support across multiple levels. The words and frameworks you choose carry weight; they signal priorities, set expectations, and define what well-being looks like in practice. That's why crosswalks—

connecting familiar language to new frameworks—can be such powerful tools for building understanding and buy-in.

> Care isn't simply a luxury; it's a core design principle. When systems support people, everyone has greater opportunities to succeed and thrive.

One guiding example is the Okanagan Charter, an international framework for health-promoting universities and colleges. I was honored to help co-create this charter, alongside global leaders in the field such as Professor Mark Dooris, Emeritus Professor of Health and Sustainability at the University of Central Lancashire in the UK. Mark has been a driving force in the health-promoting universities movement, playing a key role in shaping the charter's vision, which continues to inspire institutions worldwide.

Although initially developed for higher education, the charter's principles apply to any organization seeking to embed health into its culture. Its first call to action, "Embed health into all aspects of campus culture, across the administration, operations, and academic mandates," includes five subcommitments. These align closely, albeit not in the same order, with the five socio-ecological levels represented in the HOW ring of the Harrington Well-Being Model.[48]

- **Personal:** 1.4 Support personal development.

- **Interpersonal:** 1.3 Generate thriving communities and a culture of well-being.

- **Organizational:** 1.5 Develop or reorient campus services.
- **Environmental:** 1.2 Create supportive campus environments.
- **Policy:** 1.1 Embed health in all campus policies.

Let's take a closer look at how you can apply each of these levels of the HOW ring. The first two fall under the broad category of individual care (personal and interpersonal), and the rest address creating a culture of care (organizational, environmental, and policy).

Nurture Personal Development

This level focuses on strengthening life skills and self-awareness, enabling individuals to take ownership of their well-being. It's not about "fixing" people; it's about fostering agency, knowledge, and readiness. Whether it's building emotional resilience, improving time management, developing financial literacy, or enhancing health literacy—right down to practical skills like boiling an egg, sewing on a button, or changing a tire, as well as interpersonal capacities like having meaningful conversations and asking hard questions—personal development equips individuals to thrive.

This is often where our traditional programming work is concentrated. However, to be truly effective, we need to go beyond program-centered approaches and focus on person-centered ones—addressing the needs of our WHO populations. While diet and exercise remain vital, overall well-being is broader and must encompass all aspects of health as well as basic life skills.

Our role is to advance readiness and self-efficacy, build on strengths, and improve health literacy to help people overcome barriers such as lack of awareness, misinformation, cognitive bias, and reluctance or apathy to change—challenges that contribute to the knowing/doing gap.

Yes, nutrition and physical activity are crucial, as are sleep and hydration, especially in today's world. Equally important are the skills to connect with others, hold meaningful conversations, resolve conflicts, find purpose and passion, live by values, experience joy, manage stress healthily, and "fail forward" with resilience. When we focus our work on the whole person, we get closer to creating cultures of well-being that genuinely support human thriving.

One of the most effective ways organizations can support individual well-being is by collaborating and co-creating with the communities they serve. Instead of delivering resources alone, invite people to be part of designing what they genuinely need. For example, many food pantries offer canned or raw foods but often overlook whether individuals have the necessary tools, knowledge, or time to prepare them. Imagine the impact if those communities were involved in shaping the support—combining food distribution with cooking demonstrations, easy recipes, or starter kits of basic utensils. When we shift from simply providing for people to partnering with them, resources become more practical, meaningful, and empowering.

Self-help builds confidence. Like the saying goes: Don't just give someone a fish, teach them how to fish…and to prepare it! This encourages independence, confidence, and long-term success.

Another example, learning how to use AI to improve decision-making can boost critical thinking, not replace it. The aim is for each person to feel equipped, capable, and motivated.

Descriptors: responsibility, determination, knowledge, skills, readiness, health literacy, energy, discovery, person

Foster Interpersonal Support

Relationships are powerful drivers of behavior. This level emphasizes the importance of trust, social norms, and shared rituals of care—what we sometimes refer to as the "bandwagon effect." Whether through peer mentoring, cohort models, employee resource groups, or team-building activities, social connection promotes wellness goals. Consider someone trying to quit smoking while their closest friends still smoke, or a student trying to eat healthier in a household that favors fast food. Individual change often relies on collective support. That is why programs like bystander training, cultural competency workshops, or peer support networks matter. They do more than build individual skills; they actively shape culture.

Descriptors: trust, communication, peer support, outreach, respect, sense of community, collegiality, kindness, intercultural competence

Enhance Organizational Practices

This level integrates well-being into daily operations through onboarding, scheduling, supervision, recognition, and data management. When well-being is part of workflows, it becomes part of culture, simply "how we do things here." The American

Medical Association's CWO guide suggests addressing what they call GROSS: Getting Rid Of Stupid Stuff[49] such as outdated tech systems, inefficient workflows, or unnecessary documentation. Left unaddressed, these minor but persistent annoyances—such as a broken vending machine or unclear signage—can accumulate, erode trust, and fuel burnout. Tackling them not only reduces daily frustrations but also signals care, restores energy, and helps build confidence in the system.

You'll also want to think broadly, even as you address the "small stuff." For example, consider planting a tree. It doesn't just add shade; it can help combat climate change, purify the air, create habitats for wildlife, reduce urban heat, and improve both physical and mental health. In a local community, it becomes a symbol of how a single intentional action can generate multiple ripple effects.

The same is true in organizations. Practices that may seem narrow, such as updating the onboarding process or redesigning faculty development, can provide wide-ranging benefits when approached through a systems lens. Inclusive design such as multilingual materials, policies that permit movement breaks, or universally accessible training does more than fix isolated issues. It reinforces equity, strengthens culture, and aligns everyday operation with a more profound commitment to well-being.

This is where building collaboration capacity across departments is crucial. It creates opportunities to share ideas, resources, and improve outcomes—for instance, between HR, dining services, counseling, and student housing. The One Mental Health initiative introduced in Chapter 4 illustrates how streamlining care entry points can enhance the student experience without overloading appointments. Think creatively. Reach out to departments.

Wellness programming must be purpose-driven—aligned with the WHY, WHO, and WHAT, not just tied to monthly observance calendars. Programs should be SMART (specific, measurable, achievable, relevant, time-bound) as well as accessible, engaging, and communicated clearly.

The main goals are to build trust and to support workers. Examples include employer-sponsored mental health resources, middle-management training to recognize and respond to distress while also supporting personal and professional growth and well-being, and feedback loops that honor employee voice.

Descriptors: culture of health, collaboration, outcomes-focused, leadership support, aligned incentives, strategic planning, training, communication, accessible, fun

Shape Supportive Environments

This level involves physical and digital design. Do your spaces show care? Are they accessible, inclusive, and calming? Are they conducive to health and well-being? Are wellness cues visible in daily life, not just on posters but also in art, walking paths, break room snacks, and digital signals? Design is not superficial; it influences behavior, belonging, and dignity.

This includes the external environment—green spaces and clean air; safe sidewalks and lighting; lactation rooms; even a tranquility garden. These signals send a message to your community: You matter here. One university created a hammock garden and nap pods. Another reorganized vending machines so healthier options are the most visible (while still leaving room for the occasional morale-boosting treat). A third transformed hallways into galleries showcasing student art. Wellness can be contagious: When people see others resting, recharging, or showing vulnerability, they're more likely to do the same.

Descriptors: determinants of health, built environment, sustainability, trigger or impulse control management, occupational health, accessibility, dignity, biophilic design

Influence Policy

Policies—whether formal (big P), such as laws, HR procedures, or bylaws, or informal (little p) like unwritten traditions or norms—shape organizational culture by determining what is rewarded, normalized, and even possible. They serve as the structural backbone that can either embed well-being into an organization's core or create unintended barriers. Here are some examples of formal policies:

- A university offering paid parental leave for all employees
- A hospital updating shift schedules to reduce fatigue-related errors
- A corporation adopting carbon-neutral procurement policies
- A school district including mental health days in its attendance policy

Informal policies are equally influential, such as a department head never scheduling meetings before 9:00 a.m., a norm of keeping cameras optional for certain virtual meetings, or a tradition of recognizing milestones to foster a sense of belonging.

Even if you do not directly create policy, you can influence it by identifying the gaps between stated values and actual practice. If you promote work-life balance, is your leave policy accessible and free from stigma? If sustainability is a stated value, are your event-planning practices aligned? There are many organizational examples.

- Replacing high-waste giveaways with sustainably sourced items
- Embedding well-being expectations into every HR policy
- Mapping walking paths or installing labyrinths to encourage movement
- Adopting tobacco-free policies
- Improving nutritional standards in vending machines
- Adjusting vacation accrual systems to promote restorative time off

Whether they are written rules or cultural norms, policies are not isolated actions; they are levers for reinforcing a culture of care. And when they are intentionally designed to align with organizational values, they can normalize well-being for everyone. Even if the term "policy" is not explicitly used in your framework, the concepts can be embedded into organizational descriptors.

Descriptors: equity, social justice, protection, clarity, inclusiveness, accountability, consistency, fairness

As you can see, bringing well-being to life requires more than good intentions or well-designed programs; it necessitates intentional systems that align with both purpose and people. Like the other levels, it's important to consider how your HOW connects with the other levels by considering these connections.

- **HOW ↔ WHY** Does our infrastructure reflect our purpose or contradict it?

- **HOW ↔ WHO** Some stakeholders navigate systems with ease; others face barriers.

- **HOW ↔ WHAT** Systems should support, not just deliver, the prioritized dimensions.

- **HOW ↔ WHEN** Do our systems support care across the continuum?

Finally, you might be wondering how an organization ensures that all five aspects of the Socio-Ecological Model are fairly represented. Here are a few simple illustrations that bring the power of HOW to life.

Local Fitness Center

- **Individual:** Personalized fitness assessment and one-on-one training, goal-tracking apps

- **Interpersonal:** Group classes, intramurals, small group personal training, and walking clubs

- **Organizational:** Member incentives, wellness challenges, satisfaction surveys

- **Environmental:** Safe, clean, inclusive design with natural lighting, motivational signage, and shower(s)

- **Policy:** Equitable pricing, accessible equipment, and inclusive policies

Supporting a Tobacco-Free Environment

- **Individual:** Providing medication to help with nicotine addiction
- **Interpersonal:** Support groups and education
- **Organizational:** Tobacco cessation hotline
- **Environmental:** Minimize places to use tobacco
- **Policy:** Tobacco and smoke-free policy

The University of Houston's Well-Being Model

The University of Houston leaders adjusted the language on their model, adding terms to align with the CoogsCARE model.[50]

- **Individual:** Personal (Self-Care)
- **Interpersonal:** Culture (Fellow Coogs)
- **Organizational:** Services (UH Cares)
- **Environmental:** Setting (UH Cares)
- **Policy:** Policy (UH Cares)

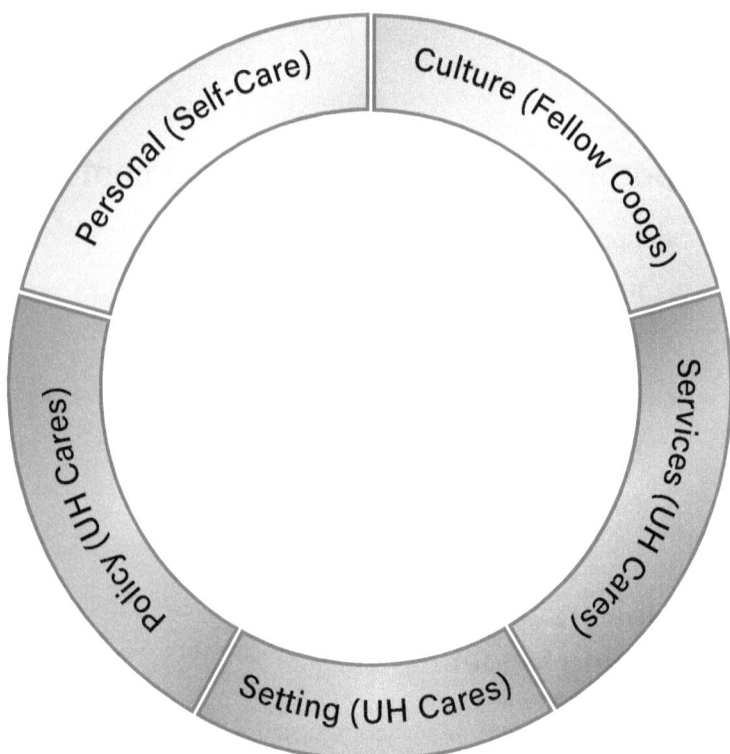

Figure 9.1: *UH HOW Ring Example: Synergy of the Levels of Change*

The HOW is grounded in the Socio-Ecological Model, which addresses nurturing individuals at personal and interpersonal levels, and creating a culture of care at organizational, environmental, and policy levels. This ensures our work integrates systems approaches in addition to supporting individuals.

Make It Yours! Make It Happen!

The HOW ring illustrates the strategies, systems, and supports that bring your well-being vision to life. Using the Socio-Ecological Model (SEM), you can identify action areas at every level—personal, interpersonal, organizational, environmental, and policy—to make sure your approach is comprehensive, coordinated, and culturally aligned.

Step One: Reflection

Reflect on how your current well-being strategies appear at each level. Consider what is working well, where there are gaps, and how you can better align your HOW with your purpose, people, and priorities.

Personal (Individual Care)

- How do you promote personal agency, skill-building, and self-efficacy?

- Do your programs reach people where they are, respecting lived experience?

Interpersonal (Social Connections)

- How can you promote belonging, peer support, and positive influence?

- Are your rituals, team norms, and group activities welcoming and safe?

Organizational (Systems & Operations)

- Where are your systems supporting well-being?
- Do your operations and processes reflect your stated values?

Environmental (Physical & Cultural Space)

- How do your spaces communicate inclusion, safety, and belonging?
- Are your environments designed to make the healthy choice the easy choice?

Policy (Formal & Informal)

- What do your policies reveal about your priorities and values?
- Are there policy adjustments, big or small, that could improve well-being for all?

Step Two: Map Your HOW

Begin identifying your categories and drafting your language for your health-promoting organization. List your strategies, systems, and actions under each SEM category as they fit within your organization. Include descriptor words that align with your organization's culture and language. These words will help you communicate your approach clearly and incorporate it into branding, messaging, and program design. You will begin to map across the rings after you have completed the WHEN ring.

PATHWAYS: HOW EXAMPLES	YOUR HOW WORDS	YOUR DESCRIPTOR CATEGORIES
Individual Care/ Personal		
Individual Care/ Interpersonal		
Culture of Care/ Organizational		
Culture of Care/ Environmental		
Culture of Care/ Policy		

Table 9.1: Pathway Language—HOW

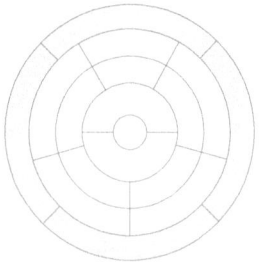

CHAPTER 10

Navigating Your Practices Through the Continuum of Care (WHEN)

Consider how most people care for their cars and even their teeth. They don't wait until the engine seizes to change the oil, or until a toothache becomes unbearable before seeing the dentist. Instead, they follow a maintenance schedule, brush and floss daily, and address small issues before they escalate into major problems. Yet in health and well-being, we often do the opposite. We wait until people are broken down or have "fallen in the river" before offering help. The WHEN ring flips that script. It's about building a proactive, comprehensive approach to care—so people get the right support at the right time, well before they reach a crisis.

Timing and intention shape your WHEN, and both are essential. There is strength in responding, and even greater power in shaping the future. Nobody wants to be sick; everyone strives to thrive and flourish. However, most wellness programs, services, and strategies focus on treatment, prevention, or risk reduction. But if you genuinely want to cultivate a culture of well-being, you need to develop systems that support people in flourishing before problems arise. That is the promise of the WHEN ring: an intentional focus on timing, care, and capacity throughout the entire process.

When the Disability Services director at one of the universities I worked at told me her team didn't belong in health and well-being efforts because the conversations focused on clinical care and the addition of upstream approaches, I had to pause. This led us to add this ring as we explored it together, which was a tremendous oversight. Their work—ensuring equitable access and responding to individual needs—was central to risk reduction.

The WHEN ring is the newest addition to the Harrington Well-Being Model. It highlights the importance of consistent care and support at all stages of health, from thriving and prevention to intervention and recovery. Are we engaging people early enough? Are we designing environments that foster lifelong well-being? Are our systems ready to respond, restore, and reconnect?

> Timing matters, as does intention. There's power in responding, and even greater power in shaping the path ahead.

To add to the complexity of a health and well-being organization, the language of the WHEN ring has many variations but the same intent, which is why I prefer to use visual metaphors as described in Chapter 5. However, it's essential to use words that resonate with your audience and reflect your organization's culture. There's no single "correct" language, but clarity and purpose are essential. That's why metaphors and crosswalks are so effective. They foster a shared understanding, even across diverse fields.

Continuum of Care

Let's explore each level using those familiar metaphors as ideas for your ring.

Upstream: Promotion and Flourishing

This level signifies proactive promotion and growth, encompassing holistic health across all dimensions. It's where you establish the conditions that keep people healthy before they approach the cliff, the metaphorical garden. It is health promotion in its purest form and by its nature salutogenic.

It's also here that much of the culture of care work takes place, across housing, nutrition, education, pay equity, green spaces, and institutional values.

Prevention: Avoiding Known Risks

Prevention involves proactive measures that reduce major health issues by promoting healthy habits and supportive environments. This is the metaphorical fence at the top of the cliff. Prevention is like a fence that helps people avoid falling in the first place through education, awareness, resilience building, vaccinations, and early screenings. It is usually midstream. Although it may have pathogenic origins, its goal is salutogenic, promoting health and well-being.

These are essential: handwashing, vaccines, screenings, and interventions save lives. Other examples include no-smoking policies, flu shot clinics, stress management classes, and campaigns to promote the normalization of mental health support.

Risk Reduction: Safety Nets

Risk reduction is like a safety net, catching people when they fall. This section covers harm reduction, early detection, accommodation, and programmatic safety nets. It is pathogenic in that it focuses on managing risk but often overlaps with access and equity.

Intervention: Crisis and Acute Care

Intervention refers to treating illness or injury, but this term can seem clinical or paternalistic. Some organizations now prefer using terms like *initiatives*, *programs*, *care delivery*, or *services* instead. This is pulling people out of the river, the ambulance, downstream at the bottom of the cliff. It includes acute medical services, therapy, hospitalization, and emergency response. It's vital lifesaving work—but costly, emotionally taxing, and not a place you want people to dwell.

Health services and counseling centers are located here. But after COVID, even clinicians avoided being labeled "pathogenic," because it implied stigma rather than support.

Recovery and Reintegration

Recovery and restoration focus on healing and helping people reenter society after setbacks. Our goal is to help them regain their footing and move toward a thriving future.

This might include peer support, academic accommodations, or structured re-onboarding at work. In many systems, this stage isn't identified, but it's essential. I often categorize it under risk reduction, though its purpose is different.

Bringing the WHEN Ring to Life

Data can be a profoundly effective way to make your WHEN clear. A favorite example comes from a health insurance company that used real numbers to illustrate the benefits of prevention, early intervention, and other healthcare.

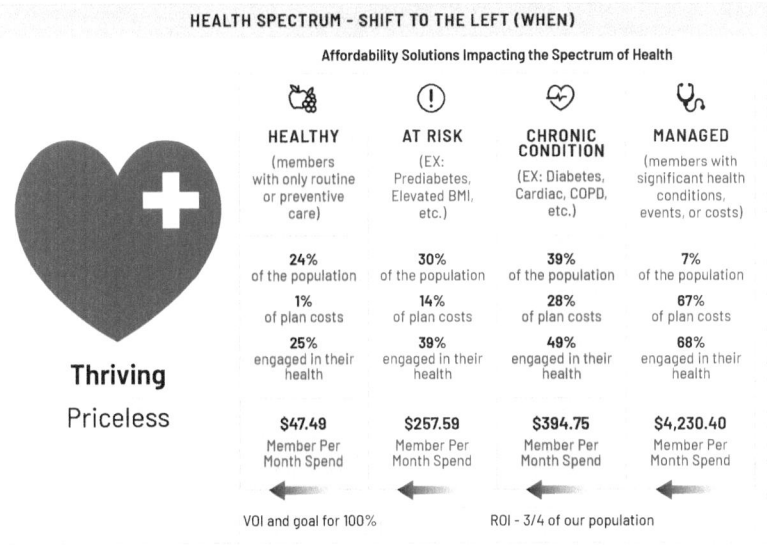

Figure 10.1: Shift to the Left Health Spectrum Example

As you can see, it outlined population segments by health status: Healthy, At Risk, Chronic Condition, and Managed.

Here are some key takeaways.

- 54% of people were healthy or at low risk, but they only accounted for 15% of the costs.

- Only 7% were in the Managed group, yet they made up 67% of the costs.

This led to our phrase "Shift to the Left." The message was clear: We must invest earlier—in prevention, thriving, and risk reduction—to avoid the human and financial toll of crisis care. Engagement usually increases with illness, but by then, it's often too late. The goal is to reverse that trend, shifting the population to the left of the graph in both the health spectrum and the cost curve, and ideally off the chart entirely, into the priceless space of thriving.

Here are a few additional examples that may resonate with your situation and organization.

Student Mental Health

- **Upstream:** Purpose campaigns and belonging initiatives

- **Prevention:** Mental health education and stress management workshops

- **Risk Reduction:** Screenings and referral systems

- **Intervention:** Counseling and emergency services

- **Recovery:** Academic accommodations and peer support

Employee Well-Being

- **Upstream:** Inclusive leadership and meaningful work
- **Prevention:** Paid time off access and burnout training
- **Risk Reduction:** Employee assistance program (EAP) visibility and mid-year check-ins
- **Intervention:** Crisis response and leave policies
- **Recovery:** Planning for return to work and reintegration

And of course, the University of Houston example and its adaptation.

University of Houston

- **Upstream/Upstream:** Promotion, and could include policies on project deadlines
- **Prevention/Midstream:** Prevention to include Department of Wellness education programs
- **Risk Reduction/Midstream:** Harm reduction to include the Dean of Students office
- **Intervention/Downstream:** Intervention to include the Counseling Center and Student Health Services
- **Recovery:** Not included in their model, but could include services by the Cougars* in Recovery department for students in recovery from addiction (*Cougars are the UH Mascot)

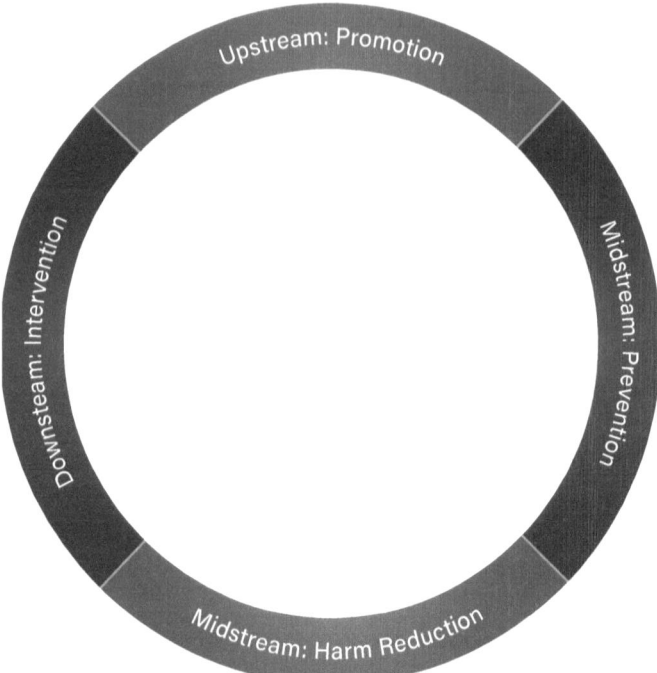

Figure 10.2: *UH WHEN Ring Example: The Continuum of Care*

The WHEN reflects the continuum of care. Instead of focusing solely on crisis or harm reduction, the health-promoting organization includes upstream efforts emphasizing prevention and long-term strategies to support people's well-being and help them thrive.

The WHEN ring demonstrates that timing isn't just about sequence—it's about strategy, fairness, and hope. It reminds you that promotion matters just as much as treatment. That safety nets are useful, but so are strong foundations. And that shifting your energy upstream helps more people stay on solid ground.

Thus as always, it's critical to consider how the WHEN ring intersects with the other rings by asking yourself key questions.

- **WHEN ↔ WHY** Are we investing where our purpose lies?

- **WHEN ↔ WHO** Are we meeting people at the right time for their needs?

- **WHEN ↔ WHAT** Are our programs effectively addressing well-being dimensions over time?

- **WHEN ↔ HOW** Are interventions layered effectively across all levels of the SEM?

By visualizing care across the full continuum—promotion, prevention, risk reduction, intervention, and recovery—you can bring clarity to complexity. You also create a shared language that invites everyone to the table, including clinicians, educators, facility staff, finance officers, HR teams, and students.

Whether you're cleaning the beach or saving the starfish, designing the system or delivering the service, the WHEN ring asks: What timing works best for your people, and what will it take to get them there?

Make It Yours! Make It Happen!

The WHEN ring is about timing and intention—creating systems that connect with people at different points along the care spectrum: upstream, prevention, risk reduction, intervention, and recovery. This activity will help you recognize your strengths, identify gaps, and develop a shared language around care.

Step One: Reflection

1. Which stage of the continuum is your organization most proficient in? Which is most overlooked?

2. How does the way you talk about care (for example, using terms like *intervention*, *prevention*, and *resilience*) influence how your services are utilized or valued?

3. What's one policy, program, or practice you could reimagine to shift further upstream?

Step Two: Choose Your Metaphor

Many teams find it easier to work with metaphors that bring the continuum of care to life to encompass upstream, prevention, risk reduction, intervention, and recovery. Use the following table to draft your own language or examples for each stage.

PRACTICES: WHEN TOPICS	YOUR TOPIC WORDS	YOUR DESCRIPTOR CATEGORIES / METAPHORS
Upstream		
Prevention		
Midstream		
Intervention		
Recovery		

Table 10.1: Practice Language—WHEN

CHAPTER 11

Assembling and Activating Your Blueprint for Successfully Building Your Health-Promoting Organization (All Together Now)

As you may have realized by now, I love a good parable. One of my favorites is the classic Indian tale about the six blind men and the elephant. They had often heard of the animal but had never experienced one in person.

One day, a truck carrying an elephant stopped on the road where the men were standing. When they heard there was an elephant in tow, they asked the driver if they could touch it and learn what kind of animal it was. The driver agreed. The first man put his hand on the elephant's side and proclaimed, "Aha! This grand animal is just like a wall."

The second man felt the elephant's tusk and corrected his friend. "Sorry, it's not like a wall in the least. It's smooth and sharp, more like a spear."

The third grabbed the elephant's trunk. "You're both wrong. The beast is long and smooth. Obviously, it's like a snake."

The fourth man put his arm around one of the elephant's legs, exclaiming, "You're all truly blind—the animal is sturdy and towering like a tree."

The fifth man was quite tall, and he grabbed the elephant's ear. "My silly friends, the animal is nothing like anything you've described. It's just like a gigantic fan."

The final man took hold of the tail. "Clearly, you all have misread this creature. It's just like a rope!"

The quarrel continued long after the truck with the elephant pulled away, with each man clinging to his interpretation. None were wrong—but without seeing the whole elephant, none were truly correct. That's what happens when we only focus on one part of creating a health-promoting organization.

Unfortunately, many organizations approach well-being in this fragmented way. Each department focuses on only a part of the whole picture. HR addresses burnout. EAP or counseling manages mental health. Facilities ensure ergonomic workspaces. The health center tracks vaccination rates. Communication handles messaging. Finance concentrates on the cost of burnout. However, until organizations create and share the full picture, the work remains fragmented and siloed, missing out on the power of collective efforts.

To truly foster a culture of well-being, we need to develop and visualize the entire system—a model that illustrates how everything is interconnected. When people see how the pieces fit together, they feel inspired, included, and motivated. When they understand their role within the system, they are more likely to participate, advocate, and lead.

In this chapter, you'll learn how to use the Harrington Well-Being Model to clearly and engagingly showcase those connection points, making the invisible visible.

The Model as a Compass: Visualizing the Intersections

Now that you have labeled your rings, it is time to see your version of the Harrington Well-Being Model in action. This is my favorite part!

The Harrington Model is not a static diagram; it's a rotating system, similar to interlocking gears or celestial rings. As a reminder, the model's concentric rings (WHO, WHAT, HOW, and WHEN) rotate around a central axis, your WHY.

> Individuals and communities (WHO) are empowered with knowledge and tools (WHAT) to make healthy choices (WHY) wherever they are (WHERE) at every stage of life (WHEN), fostering a healthier, more vibrant tomorrow.

Each ring rotates independently around that WHY bullseye, aligning its priorities based on your focus. A program or initiative may emphasize one audience, dimension, or level of care over another. But as the rings spin, you can discover intersections and new ways to address a topic of interest. This is where the magic happens. This is where strategy aligns with culture, programs with policies, and efforts with intention.

Additionally, each ring's sections represent strategic levers with their own descriptor words and unique subsections or segments, such as different audiences. Here are brief descriptions of each ring as a reminder.

- **WHY Ring:** This anchors all efforts by clarifying the reason behind them, such as ensuring successful graduates. Purpose is the guiding star that shapes vision and direction.

- **WHO Ring:** These are the individuals and stakeholders involved, including internal members, such as employees, students, and faculty, as well as external ones, including families and community partners. People are the heart of the system.

- **WHAT Ring:** These represent the central topics or dimensions of well-being that organizations decide to emphasize, such as physical, emotional, spiritual, social, and professional. Priorities shape the focus of the work.

- **HOW Ring:** This reflects the methods and levels of intervention, often grounded in the Socio-Ecological Model. Practices can occur at the individual, interpersonal, organizational, environmental, or policy level, shaping how strategies are implemented.

- **WHEN Ring:** This illustrates the timing, sequence, and continuum of actions, from upstream promotion and primary prevention to midstream support services, downstream care, and recovery or reintegration. The path shapes momentum and sustainability.

These segments are interconnected; they are designed to align, intersect, and rotate to fit a specific context, strategy, or moment across the rings. Their true strength lies in viewing them not as separate parts but as interactive layers that support each other.

Think of it like a combination lock: When the rings align correctly, they unlock strategic clarity, system synergy, and coordinated action. This alignment isn't static; it's dynamic. The rings rotate based on needs, data, and opportunities. When they align perfectly—such as addressing spiritual well-being (WHAT) for faculty (WHO) through interpersonal connections (HOW) at the prevention level (WHEN)—you activate a powerful, timely system intervention.

Visualizing those intersections across rings shifts how teams plan, collaborate, and act. Rotating the rings helps you adapt to new health data (for example, stress levels rising post-pandemic), emerging challenges (such as financial insecurity), or organizational priorities (retention or belonging initiatives). By rotating the rings, you identify new connection points and emergent strategies, like discovering new constellations in a moving sky.

Examples in Action: Visualizing Intersections at the University of Houston

Magic happens at the intersection points, creating alignment and excitement as people start to see their roles within a health-promoting organization. It guides the assessment of overlaps and gaps—whether you are meeting goals related to the WHY and the WHO, planning, and evaluation.

By bringing the rings together, you create a shared story. Suddenly, within a university setting, mental health services aren't just offering counseling; they become student-centered, caring, and personalized interventions rooted in a mission to help students "Be Well to Do Well."

For example, the facilities staff recognized that broken sidewalks posed physical and environmental risks to everyone, especially those in wheelchairs, and that repairing them quickly can serve as a strategy to promote overall well-being. They were excited to see that they had an important role in supporting organizational well-being.

Tobacco-free policies exemplify population-level, behavioral midstream interventions. Showing these layers together paints a holistic picture and involves everyone in the mission.

Example #1:
Counseling and Psychological Services (CAPS)

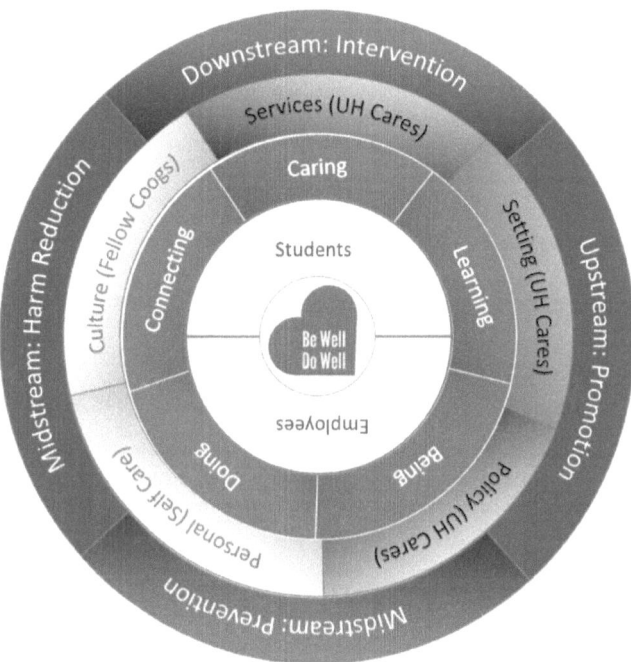

Figure 11.1: UH Counseling and Psychological Services (CAPS): Intersectionality Example

Here are three real-world examples from the University of Houston that demonstrate how the model promotes clarity and connection.

- **WHY** → "Be Well to Do Well" Supporting student mental health contributes directly to academic success

- **WHO** → Students (since CAPS is a student-fee-funded program)

- **WHAT** → Caring, or emotional well-being (mental health, resilience, stress skills)
- **HOW** → While these services offer individual support, in this context, they are provided as services
- **WHEN** → Downstream; focused on intervention and recovery at the time of need

Rotate the Rings

When focusing on student counseling, rotate…

1. Students to the top of the WHO ring
2. Caring to the top of the WHAT ring
3. Services (UH Cares) to the top of the HOW ring
4. Downstream/Intervention to the top of the WHEN ring

This framing helped CAPS employees demonstrate how their work aligns with the university's mission and values. It also reinforced that mental health support is more than clinical care—it's a strategic contributor to academic success and student well-being.

Example #2:
Repairing Broken Sidewalks

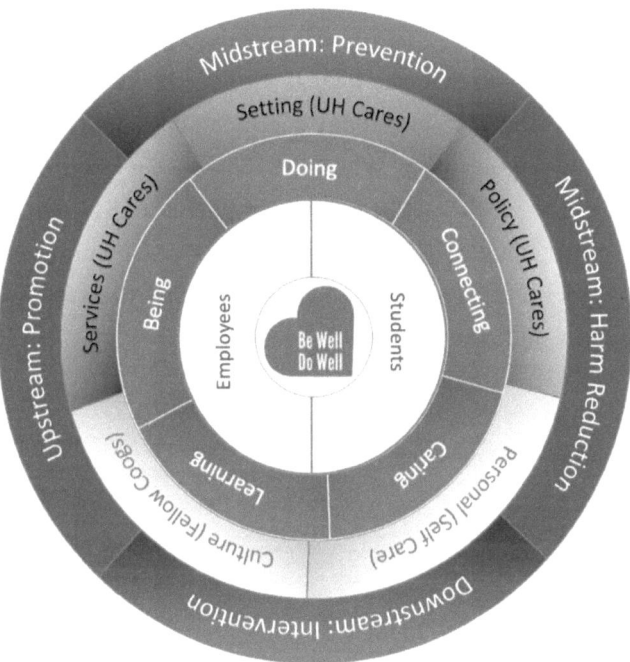

Figure 11.2: UH Broken Sidewalks Intersectionality Example

- **WHY** → "Be Well to Do Well" Safety and accessibility is essential to being well and doing well

- **WHO** → Students, employees, visitors—everyone on campus

- **WHAT** → Physical/doing (safety, mobility)

- **HOW** → Setting (UH Cares) as these are environmental and built environment changes

- **WHEN** → Midstream: Prevention, preventing injury and falls

Rotate the Rings

Rotate similarly so that the WHO, WHAT, HOW, and WHEN rings align. This isn't just about pavement. It's about well-being and shared responsibility. When the rings were aligned, the facilities team saw their role in promoting safety, equity, and health, not just managing repairs. It also encouraged collaboration among other departments, including operations, disability services, health promotion, and risk management.

Example #3:
Tobacco-Free Policies

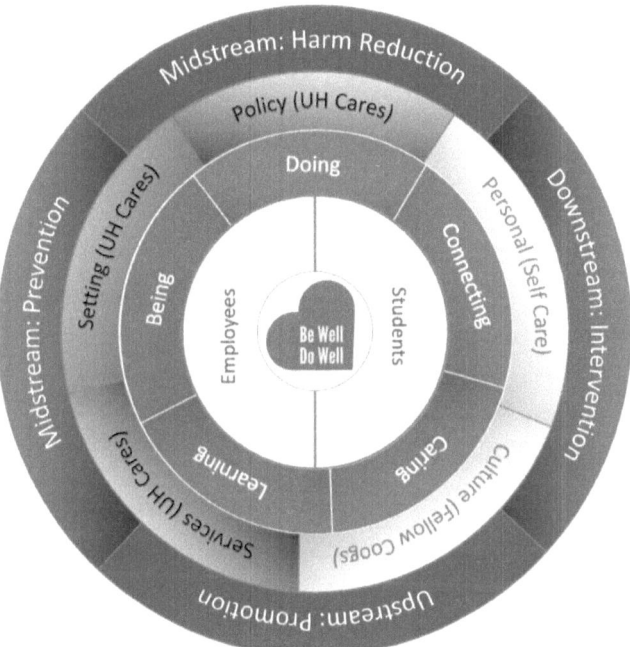

Figure 11.3: UH Tobacco-Free Intersectionality Example

- **WHY** → "Be Well to Do Well" Supporting long-term health for all community members
- **WHO** → Students and employees
- **WHAT** → Physical well-being (tobacco-free environments)
- **HOW** → Policy-level strategy
- **WHEN** → Midstream: Harm reduction

Rotate the Rings

Again, align the rings. Policy decisions can sometimes feel abstract or disconnected from daily well-being. This model clarified the alignment and impact, helping leaders understand that policies like tobacco-free zones aren't about restrictions; they're about equity, safety, and long-term health.

It's Time to Activate the Model

Sometimes I'm asked "Now what? I've identified the components of my ring, adapted my model, and see the cool intersectionality. What's next?" Here's where your model shifts from theory to action. The rotating rings aren't just a visual—they're your show-and-tell engagement piece. Use them to spark conversations, guide strategy, and support assessment and evaluation through crosswalks and other tools. These applications work especially well for strategic planning, retreats, Certified Healthy application prep, and council onboarding.

People love visuals. One of my favorite ways to present this is by sharing a tangible, movable 3D model along with a PowerPoint presentation for stakeholders. Consider creating a model with laminated ring layers that can rotate and be held in place with a brass brad.

Figure 11.4: *3D Example of an Early Version of the UH Model*

The model helps people see themselves in the bigger picture and engage more deeply. I've watched eyes light up when someone recognizes their work in the intersectionality. They see alignment with other organizations, and suddenly their role feels bigger.

These real-world "aha" moments demonstrate that well-being isn't limited to one department; it's everywhere. Everyone has a role, just as they did during the movements for safety, quality, and diversity. This is also the ideal time to evaluate whether you're using language that resonates, empowers, and unites within your organization.

When individuals and departments can see where their work connects to the larger vision, several powerful things happen.

- They feel ownership. "That's not just a wellness thing—that's MY thing."
- They see impact. "Now I get why my program matters in the bigger picture."
- They collaborate more. "Let's partner up to amplify both our efforts."
- They find identity. "This is the kind of culture I want to be part of."
- They stop reinventing the wheel. "I didn't know you were doing that. Let's link up."

Department Alignment One-Pager

A simple yet effective way to align departmental work with your well-being strategy is to create a one-page executive summary. Include the model graphic (similar to the UH example), layered descriptor words, the well-being mission and vision, and possibly priorities or key stakeholders. It can be shared with the C-suite and the well-being committee—during onboarding, retreats, or strategic realignments—to encourage reflection, recognize patterns, and position each department as part of the larger system.

You can use the one-pager for key reflection questions such as these.

- What well-being needs are most relevant to our people?
- How are we currently supporting those needs?
- Which ring(s) does our work intersect?
- What opportunities exist for collaboration, enhancement, or innovation?

Additionally, you can ask departments or teams to rate their alignment with each ring or segment on a scale of 1–5, then shade the segments to show where their energy is focused. This visual snapshot helps identify collaboration opportunities, compare teams or campuses, track year-over-year progress, and generate ideas for new strategies.

Expanding the Power of Intersectionality into Assessment and Planning

As you can tell by now, your Harrington Well-Being Model isn't just for display; it's built for action. You can bring it to life through strategic planning, operational assessment, program development, communication, and cultural transformation.

When organizations embrace intersections, the WHY is not just stated but actively lived across multiple areas; the WHO becomes clearer, more inclusive, and better supported; the WHAT transforms into actionable steps rather than abstract ideas; the HOW fosters sustainable, layered change; and the WHEN ensures ongoing continuity and responsiveness over time.

Once people recognize the model's power, the next step is to apply it to make meaningful changes.

- Make the invisible visible.
- Facilitate cross-functional collaboration.
- Highlight gaps and overlaps.
- Promote shared language and ownership.
- Support both big-picture strategy and everyday action.

What makes this model truly transformative is its intersectionality—the way the rings interconnect and support each other, not just visually but also in practice. Beyond serving as a rotating visual, the model's components act as a blueprint for assessment, planning, and evaluation. They guide leaders in thinking through strategy from concept to implementation.

For example, the WHO and WHAT rings work together to help customize programs for specific audiences and dimensions. The HOW ring allows the same strategy to be adapted at individual, interpersonal, environmental, and policy levels. The WHEN ring ensures efforts include prevention and recovery, avoiding a narrow focus and ensuring continuity across the full continuum of care.

Using the model in assessment helps identify areas for improvement. For example, if all your energy goes into intervention, such as crisis counseling, EAP support, or emergency healthcare, you're not wrong. But you could be missing opportunities to prevent those crises in the first place. Recovery services are just as important to help people not just survive but thrive again. On the other hand, if all your programs focus on wellness education (upstream/prevention) and there's no infrastructure to respond to risk or support healing, people may feel unsupported when they need help most. Using the model in assessment helps visualize that and helps identify leverage points, areas where a small intervention can create a significant impact; build cohesive campaigns, such as a theme that links a specific population, dimension, level, and point in time; and break silos, by fostering collaboration among departments around shared goals and strategies.

Two Crosswalk Tools to Map and Show Intersections

In two previous roles, I created assessment planning tools to identify gaps aligned with organizational priorities. One of the most effective methods was a planning matrix, which visually maps how work intersects within the Harrington Well-Being Model's rings.

A practical example comes from the University of Houston, where an assessment document, first adopted by the Wellness department, is now being adapted for use across the entire Health and Well-Being Portfolio. The Wellness staff welcomed it wholeheartedly, using it to direct both planning and evaluation.

You can develop a similar tool by designing a spreadsheet or visual chart with rows for programs, campaigns, or strategies and columns for the WHO, WHAT, HOW, and WHEN rings. Mark an X or use color-coding where each element applies. This straightforward visual quickly highlights which strategies are overused, underdeveloped, or ready for better alignment—making it easier to balance efforts and maximize impact.

Another organization used a similar tool to assess current needs and decide where efforts should be amplified, activated, innovated, or scaled back. This method helped teams choose which well-being programs to expand, launch, redesign, or discontinue and was especially useful during retreats or when consolidating scattered wellness initiatives into a unified strategy.

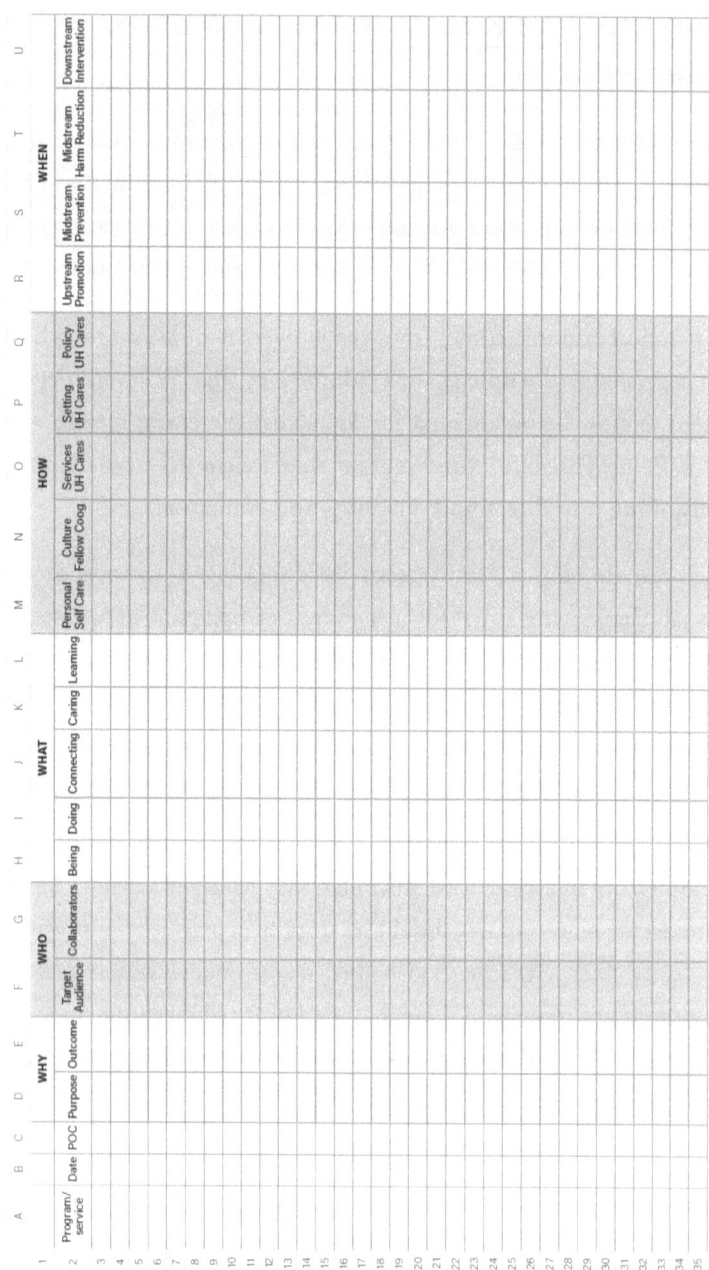

Table 11.1: Assessment Example

Step-By-Step

1. Select a well-being dimension in the words of the organization. For example, Physical/Doing.

2. In the left column, list the five HOW levels from the Socio-Ecological Model using your organization's chosen words.

3. Across the top row, list the four action categories—Amplify, Activate, Innovate, or Reduce.

4. In each cell, note existing programs or desired initiatives.

FOCUS	AMPLIFY	ACTIVATE	INNOVATE	REDUCE
Personal				
Interpersonal				
Organizational				
Environmental				
Policy				

Table 11.2: Assessment Tool Example

Mapping programs this way provides teams with a clear visual of resource distribution, gaps, and new opportunities. Any of the rings can be cross-referenced in this way. For example, a similar table could be something like this. (Note that this example does not have to include a column for Reduce.)

FOCUS	AMPLIFY	ACTIVATE/RE-IGNITE	INNOVATE
Personal	• Healthy eating • RD classes and promotion	• Back to Basics campaign • Encourage preventive screening and know your numbers • Chronic disease counseling (RD and CDE/RN ed.) • Onsite fitness classes	• Back to Basics campaign • Obesity specialist physician training • Aligned benefits such as family forming • NP for all stages of women's health • Sponsored activities
Interpersonal	• Fortify, increase, and market ambassadors	• Health condition support groups • Activate ambassadors	• Activated ambassador and messaging • Connection groups for walking, riding, or Frisbee
Organizational	• Market EMC and Wellness services • Support benefits and ComPsych resources	• Nutrisystem or Weight Watchers • Formalized walking paths; fun stairwells and encouraging signage • Classes such as yoga and boot camps • Cooking classes • Strong collaboration and referrals internal to HR and others • Community/affinity groups around activities, meals, hobbies • Activate purposeful ambassador challenges • Activate Annual Enrollment with PERMA survey and onsite physicals	• Amazon or other prepared family meals • Food pantry? Or strong collaboration • Encourage walking meetings and standing desks • Connection with services • One stop shop web platform and physical site • Coordinated and intentional surveys – HA, QoL, needs • Collaboration with other areas such as the Food Bank • Care coordinators for effective referrals and follow-ups • Women's health NP, CDE • Kindness coins
Environmental	• Healthy food options • Massage chairs • Nursing rooms	• Healthy eating opportunities 24/7 • Maps of walking with mile markers; fortify stairwells; maps of fun places to see • Peloton or other fitness/activity rooms	• Stock lounges with healthy food options • Cost adjustments for vending machines • Activate many places to eat, rest, and be active • Tobacco and vape free • Nap pods, green space/community garden, gyms for all
Policy			• Healthy food options 24/7 and at meetings • Remove McDonalds and smoking areas

Figure 11.3: Program Planning Tool Example

Rotating Ring Planner: Planning from Scratch

Whether starting from scratch or modifying existing plans, this approach proves useful. It encourages cross-disciplinary thinking from the outset. Use the model and its intersectionality to answer these questions and create initiative "recipes." Select one element from each ring and develop a customized strategy. This alignment illustrates how a specific program can connect with five strategic touchpoints, each boosting the others.

Step-By-Step

1. **WHY** → What's our purpose or value? What truly motivates our work?

2. **WHO** → Who are we trying to reach? Who are we including, and who might be left out (for example, early-career staff or students with different abilities)?

3. **WHAT** → Which well-being dimensions are being addressed? What do we mean by "well-being" in this moment?

4. **HOW** → How can change occur across systems? What level(s) of the Socio-Ecological Model can we include?

5. **WHEN** → When should we intervene, prevent, or promote? Where does this fall on the continuum?

Example: Addressing mental health for first-generation students

1. **WHO** → First-generation students

2. **WHAT** → Emotional and social well-being

3. **HOW** → Interpersonal level via peer mentoring

4. **WHEN** → Primary prevention

5. **WHY** → Belonging and compassion

The power comes from the intersections. When rings and their subsections align, you create these kinds of results:

- **Precision impact:** Interventions are more effective because they're relevant to both the audience and the dimension.

- **Cross-functional planning:** Teams from different departments can rally around the same goal from various angles.

- **De-siloed culture:** Seeing overlap naturally encourages collaboration.

To demonstrate the model's power across various settings, the following two detailed hypothetical examples illustrate how to create a program from scratch, considering the model—one in a workplace and one in a community—highlighting the richness of intersectionality and how these tools help drive alignment and engagement. It also encourages broader thinking about how to address the challenge by identifying and aligning different sectors of each ring.

Workplace Example: Enhancing Sleep Health in a Manufacturing Plant

Challenge: High rates of fatigue, safety incidents, and absenteeism among night-shift workers

- **WHY** → Safety, performance, family balance
- **WHO** → Night-shift employees, line supervisors, senior leaders
- **WHAT** → Physical, emotional, and professional well-being
- **HOW** →
    - Individual: Sleep hygiene education and one-on-one coaching
    - Interpersonal: Peer buddy system for accountability
    - Organizational: Revised scheduling to reduce consecutive night shifts
    - Environmental: Rest pods for scheduled breaks
    - Policy: Annual sleep assessment during wellness exams
- **WHEN** →
    - Upstream: Proactive education
    - Midstream: Screening during high-stress times
    - Downstream: Treatment and accommodation for sleep apnea

Result: A branded campaign that integrated health, performance, and values. It promoted cross-departmental ownership and led to a measurable decrease in injuries and absenteeism. The rings were aligned to create a systems-level impact across safety, retention, and morale, resulting in a branding campaign that was adopted across departments.

Community Example: Fostering Food Security in an Urban Neighborhood

Challenge: Food deserts, rising chronic disease, and community disconnection

- **WHY** → Equitable access to live a healthy life
- **WHO** → Low-income families, elderly residents, local food providers
- **WHAT** → Physical, social, and financial well-being
- **HOW** →
    - Individual: Cooking classes
    - Interpersonal: Peer-led meal-planning groups
    - Organizational: Markets distributing fresh produce
    - Environmental: Gardens and transit access
    - Policy: Zoning changes to attract grocers and farmers markets
- **WHEN** →
    - Upstream: Gardening programs in communities
    - Midstream: Integrated food pantries
    - Downstream: Chronic disease management with food access

Result: What began as a food pantry expansion evolved into a citywide initiative, featuring a shared vision, cobranded messaging, and unified data dashboards across education, housing, and public health. It connected multiple city departments, nonprofits, and residents into a familiar story—and used visual crosswalk tools to monitor progress and engagement.

Make It Yours! Make It Happen!

By now, you've explored each ring of the Harrington Well-Being Model and have seen how they connect. This is your moment to move from theory to practice, using the model not just as a framework to study, but also as a living tool for planning, evaluating, and transforming your organization's approach to well-being.

Whether you're working through this solo as a wellness advocate or facilitating with a team, the following exercise is designed to spark insight, surface opportunities, and guide your next step.

Part One: Reflection

Pause here to reflect. Use these questions to examine where you are today, where alignment exists, and where opportunities are waiting to be activated.

Alignment and Gaps

- Where is your organization already aligned across the five rings?
- What's working well? How do you know?

- Where are your current gaps, overlaps, or missed opportunities?

Clarity and Communication

- How well do people in your organization understand the purpose (WHY) of your well-being work?

- Could the model help communicate this more clearly to your leaders, colleagues, or stakeholders?

- What's one way you could visually share the model within the next month?

Roles and Ownership

- Where are people struggling to see themselves in the work of well-being?

- What tools or approaches could help them find their place?

- How could you use the model to onboard a new committee member or engage a skeptical leader?

Activation and Application

- Where could you integrate the model into existing processes, such as strategic planning, program review, training, or retreats?

- How might you use the crosswalk tool, alignment map, or assessment wheel with your teams?

- What's one low-hanging fruit you could implement next week?

Branding and Identity

- What language or visual could become a consistent cue for your culture of well-being?

- How might you personalize the rings to reflect your brand, values, or the people you care about?

- Where could you place the model (literally or figuratively), so it becomes part of daily conversation?

Growth and Sustainability

- How will you revisit the model over time?

- What system or rhythm could help you realign, reflect, and reengage?

Part Two: Action

Reflection is powerful, but only action creates change. Use the model as more than just a visual—make it your blueprint for building a culture of well-being.

1. **Visualize:** Rotate your rings to identify key intersections—for example, between purpose and people, priorities, pathways, and practices.

2. **Engage:** Choose your first ally or department. Share your model and show how their work connects to the bigger picture.

3. **Apply:** Use a tool (3D model, crosswalk matrix, or department one-pager) to map current efforts and more easily spot gaps or overlaps.

4. **Implement:** Select one initiative to align or adapt using insights from your model.

5. **Evaluate:** Decide what success will look like for both outcomes and culture as you shift and expand your focus.

6. **Repeat:** Revisit the model regularly, rotate the rings, and invite new partners into the conversation.

SECTION THREE

MAKING IT HAPPEN: PRACTICAL TOOLS FOR ADVANCING YOUR HEALTH-PROMOTING ORGANIZATION

Now that you've learned how to use the Harrington Well-Being Model, it's time to turn your blueprint into action. Just like any construction project, you need both a clear plan and the right tools to bring it to life. Whether you're a solo champion or part of a cross-functional well-being team, the information and practical tools in this section are designed to help you create alignment, build synergy, strengthen communication, measure impact, and ensure sustainability for your organization and for yourself.

These chapters are designed with your reality in mind: time is limited, stakeholders are diverse, and change can feel overwhelming. That's why the focus is on strategies that are proven, practical, adaptable, and empowering—so you can start with what works, customize it for your context, and build from there.

The tools in these chapters are intentionally affordable, easy to use, and designed to become self-sustaining—crucial when priorities shift. They focus on helping you think differently and applying what you already know in new, practical ways. That's the beauty of a well-being culture: When it's part of everyday work, progress keeps moving forward even during changes.

As you move through the rest of this book, be kind to yourself. Remember, you aren't alone—well-being belongs to everyone and is most successful when it's a collective effort. And you don't have to do everything at once. Begin with what you can handle—one task, one project, one conversation—and allow it to expand. And finally, your story matters. How you communicate your model, engage others, and measure your impact influences how the culture changes. It's how you make it happen!

CHAPTER 12

Develop Your Well-Being Team

A culture of well-being requires just that—a culture—and that is built of and by people.

One day, while working on a jigsaw puzzle with my daughter, I realized it mirrored the state of organizational well-being at work. All the pieces were there—some already in place along the edges, others forming connections in the middle through shared colors or themes—while many more still waited, spread across the mat or tucked away in the box, ready to be discovered.

Just as it is when you're putting together a puzzle, your role is to start building the border, connect what you can, and search for those still waiting to be found. What needs to be amplified, activated, or innovated (or de-activated)? Like puzzle pieces, the elements of a well-being culture already exist. You are not starting entirely from scratch. Instead, you're revealing and uniting the network of people and efforts that already exist, breaking down silos and empowering everyone to work together toward the shared purpose and goal, each with their unique role (interconnectivity). Together, you will create a mosaic of care and connections. And when people see how they fit into the bigger picture, they're more likely to engage, contribute, and lead. Your job is to help them see that picture.

Just as earlier generations took a systems approach to safety during the industrial age, and later advanced quality improvement through models like total quality management (TQM), Six Sigma, and PDCA (Plan, Do, Check, Act), which remain valuable today, followed by the expansion of diversity, equity, and inclusion (DEI), the next frontier is well-being.

These shifts often begin within a single department or with one passionate leader, but their lasting success depends on everyone becoming responsible. Safety is everyone's job. Quality is everyone's job. Well-being and belonging are everyone's job. Your role is to help them see it, believe it, and live it.

> A culture of well-being doesn't need unlimited funding. It requires focus, alignment, curiosity, and strong relationships, as together you target early wins while keeping your core purpose in mind.

Find Your Collaborators

Start with a simple question: Who else cares about this? Begin by identifying existing efforts and potential allies. Build your team, and create meaningful connections. Arrange strategic conversations, whether in formal meetings or casual coffee chats, to listen, learn, and ask thoughtful questions. Look for those already working on related issues, your early supporters, and trusted influencers. Consider who else benefits from the outcome or has the power to help drive change. For example, parents and families are often powerful champions for individual health—whether it's parents of college students advocating for campus well-being or families encouraging healthy habits at home.

A key part of your early momentum comes from this kind of exploration and relationship-building. Your goal is to break down silos, align goals, co-create shared strategies, and boost organizational capacity. Remember, silos don't usually form because people don't care; they form because people care deeply about their own areas. Your role is to connect that care to a shared vision.

Start by talking with your direct supervisor, your immediate team, and any members of the well-being or engagement committee. Schedule one-on-one meetings to find out what they value, what they need, and what they'd love to see changed. Ask open-ended questions like…

- What's working well?
- What's getting in the way?
- What are the main needs or stressors?
- Who else should I be talking to?

Bring your new Harrington Well-Being Model draft to spark curiosity and inspire fresh ideas. Share the vision—not as a rigid prescription, but as an open invitation to explore possibilities together. Paint a picture of what's possible when each person's work is connected to a bigger purpose. Show where their current efforts already align with the model, and encourage them to identify additional connections you might have missed.

As you listen, watch for the themes, shared values, and common language that naturally emerge. Pay close attention to the descriptor words people use when they talk about well-being, success, or workplace culture. Are these words reflected in your model draft? Do they align with your organization's goals? If not, are they still the right words, or is there a gap that needs to be filled? The language you identify here will be crucial for gaining support and shaping your communication plan.

This discovery phase is also an essential part of your well-being SWOT analysis,[51] a useful method for identifying these areas:

- Strengths (internal assets and advantages)
- Weaknesses (internal challenges or limitations)
- Opportunities (external possibilities for growth or impact)
- Threats (external risks or barriers)

As you gather insights, start noticing patterns. Where are the bright spots that could be enhanced or expanded? What recurring pain points emerge in conversations? Where do you see untapped opportunities for alignment, collaboration, or innovation?

Finally, don't underestimate the influence of informal leaders—the people without formal titles who nonetheless shape culture, influence peers, and get things done. They're often the "connective tissue" that helps initiatives thrive behind the scenes, without seeking recognition. Ensure that you include them in these conversations, listen to their ideas, and invite them into the process. These trusted connectors could become your most effective champions for change.

Every organization has a unique structure. You might be part of a complex matrix system, a global company, a nonprofit organization, or a regional business. Regardless of the setup, look across departments: Consider human resources, employee experience, learning and development, facilities, operations, finance, safety, communications, and IT. Identify leaders who are already dedicated to employee satisfaction, productivity, innovation, or workplace culture. These individuals are your well-being allies, even if they don't hold that specific title.

Explore your company's intranet, organizational charts, or project directories. Review employee resource groups, affinity networks, or cross-functional committees. Identify individuals or teams already working on complementary initiatives—whether it's resilience, equity, sustainability, professional development, or belonging. Connect with them.

Begin developing your collaborator or partner network not by requesting buy-in but by asking what matters to them. That's how shared ownership starts. That's how your momentum grows.

When talking about partnerships, the term *collaboration* is often used, and it's generally understood as inviting someone to your table. However, meaningful systems change requires more than extending an invitation to what you are doing—it's about building the table together. While collaboration is metaphorically inviting someone to the dance, integration is actually dancing together. True integration extends beyond coordination to encompass a shared vision, collaborative planning, aligned goals, and common metrics. It requires sustained trust, transparency, and a commitment to collective impact.

Integration also means using purposeful language that bridges perspectives, identifies common ground, and turns mutual respect into joint action. It's not about compromise for the sake of agreement; it's about co-creating solutions that reflect the strengths and capacities of every partner. This approach transforms a collection of parallel efforts into an aligned force, making well-being not just one department's responsibility but everyone's shared mission.

As I've emphasized throughout this book, language matters. When I was working with health and counseling teams on one campus, I learned that the word *integration* was triggering anxiety for some, especially counselors who feared being absorbed or overshadowed by others' work. That was their interpretation of the word. So we paused and unpacked the language together, shifting the focus toward partnership rather than assimilation. That reframing built trust.

A valuable resource at this stage is this Collaboration Spectrum visual found on the Collective Impact Forum.[52] This framework illustrates a progression of relationships—beginning with competition and moving through coexistence, communication, coordination, true collaboration, and ultimately, full integration. It can be a powerful, eye-opening tool to help visualize where your current partnerships fall on that spectrum and to identify the direction in which you'd like them to grow. It's particularly useful for reflecting on trust, alignment, and shared purpose.

The University of Houston has effectively used this tool not just as a partnership checklist but also as a guide for building meaningful relationships, rather than just managing programs. They incorporated the spectrum into their assessment and program-planning processes under the WHO category of the assessment tool in Chapter 2. By mapping each initiative to its current position on the spectrum, they could track progress toward deeper collaboration and stronger cross-functional alignment. Their clear measurable outcome was to show a visible shift to the right along the spectrum over time, where appropriate.

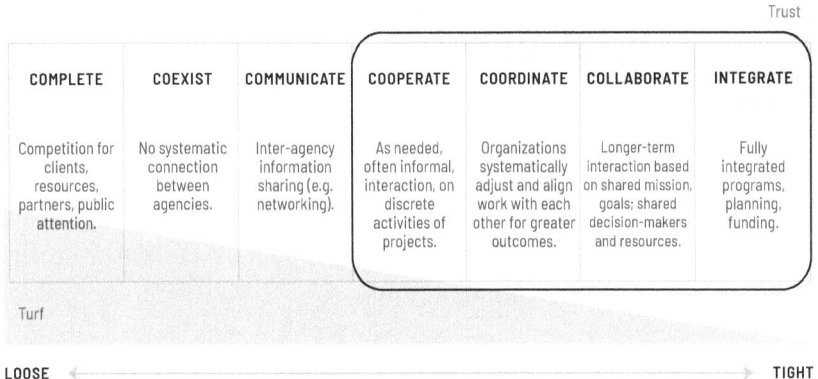

Figure 12.1: Collaboration Spectrum[53]

When used thoughtfully, the Collaboration Spectrum can inspire candid conversations, reveal hidden opportunities for teamwork, and build a shared vision for working together toward greater impact.

Putting Collaboration into Action

Once you've had your stakeholder meetings and gathered initial SWOT insights, begin synthesizing what you've heard. Look for patterns across teams and dimensions of well-being.

- Which dimensions are already strong?
- Which ones are being underserved or overlooked?
- Where do programs overlap or operate in silos?
- Where are natural intersections and opportunities for alignment?

For example, in one organization, we discovered that three separate departments were offering similar training: one focused on conflict de-escalation, another on psychological safety, and a third on mental health first aid. Individually, each effort was strong. Together, they formed a unified strategy for creating safe and supportive environments. This demonstrates the power of a systems approach.

Begin connecting the dots. Where can alignment strengthen impact? Where might collaboration reduce duplication? Where do people want to help but feel disconnected?

Cultivate relationships and capacity. Having conversations helps people feel seen, which encourages them to show up authentically and work toward shared success. Relationships form the foundation of culture, and culture determines the success or failure of your well-being initiatives.

As you engage stakeholders, listen carefully for their WIIFM (What's In It For Me?). Identify where your shared goals align. For example, if human resources focuses on recruitment and retention, demonstrate how well-being supports those outcomes. If the executive leaders are concerned about healthcare costs or absenteeism, explore how upstream strategies can help. When others see how a health-promoting organization advances their goals—in their language—they're more likely to get involved. In time, these small bridges lead to significant breakthroughs.

When attitude, expectation, and perception align, the work feels like gears meshing. Attitude sets the tone, expectation sets the standard, and perception shapes what people believe is possible. With a hopeful, accountable stance; clear, achievable goals; and visible evidence to match, trust builds. Meetings become shorter, resistance diminishes, and small wins serve as signals—not accidents. That's the power of alignment: Energy turns into momentum, momentum into culture, and culture into lasting results.

So as you build your collaborator map and expand your relationships, remember: You're not just gathering allies—you're co-creating a movement. Keep it real. Keep it inclusive. And keep going.

Building the Committee (or Coalition)

Once you've mapped your organizational landscape, it's time to formalize your team. This becomes your internal well-being committee, or strategic coalition. It should reflect a broad cross-section of your organization, involving departments such as human resources, occupational health, communications, facilities, safety, finance, benefits, employee resource groups, learning and development, and other units that influence the employee experience.

- Be intentional in how you invite members. Clearly communicate that this isn't a typical wellness program committee—it's a systems-level alignment team. Their role is to…

- Establish a shared vision for well-being.
- Define organizational priorities and outcomes.
- Identify and align current and emerging initiatives.
- Monitor progress and measure impact.
- Coordinate messaging and embed culture.

This committee might form smaller working groups or task forces focused on key priorities, such as psychological safety, physical health, belonging, or career growth. For example, at UH, we established the Houston Nutrition Collective to support the needs fulfilled by the food pantry, consisting of faculty, students, and student affairs professionals. The collective addressed…

- **Individual knowledge:** Nutrition education and habit-building

- **Organizational support:** Tackling food insecurity with benefit and subsidy programs

- **Environmental access:** Availability of healthy food across shifts and locations

This committee and the working groups should consist of people with both passion and influence—those who are ready to lead implementation, not just participate in discussion. That's how you build momentum and create meaningful change.

Start with WHY

Because it may take several meetings to bring this team together, begin by exploring each of the model's rings, starting with WHY.

One of the first and most important agenda items for your committee may be to define what well-being means for your organization. This might happen during the initial meeting, or it may take time and thoughtful discussion across several. That's okay. The goal is to create a shared understanding that reflects your organization's values, purpose, and people.

As previously noted, the World Health Organization defines health as "a state of complete physical, mental, and social well-being" and not merely "the absence of disease or infirmity." While this serves as a valuable foundation, your organization's definition should be specific, meaningful, and actionable within your unique context. What does well-being look like here? What does it feel like to work in a place that truly supports it? The answers to these questions will shape a shared understanding that guides strategy, aligns efforts, and brings your vision to life.

For example, while I was at the American Nurses Association, we created the following definition to guide our work: "A Healthy Nurse is one who takes care of their personal health, safety, and wellness, and lives life to their fullest capacity—physically, mentally, spiritually, and professionally—so they can be a better role model, educator, and advocate." We also added these five pillars to define our WHY further.

- Calling to care
- Priority to self-care
- Opportunity to role model

- Responsibility to educate
- Authority to advocate

Your version might emphasize vitality, purpose, connection, safety, belonging, or growth. The words you select will act as your guiding star anchoring strategy, shaping messaging, and aligning every initiative. And when done well, your WHY becomes something your entire workforce can see themselves in and rally around.

Let the conversation flow. Invite reflection. Encourage your coalition to think beyond programs to culture and experience. Ask questions like these.

- What does thriving look here—for individuals, teams, and organizations?
- What does caring for our people mean, beyond simply managing them?
- How does well-being connect to our mission, values, and long-term impact?
- If someone were describing our culture at its best, what words would they use?

These conversations are more than simply wordsmithing; they are opportunities to spark shared ownership and collective energy. What will your definition be? Invite your committee to co-create one that feels authentic, actionable, and inspiring. And remember, it may take more than one meeting to get there—some people need time to reflect, process, and bring their best ideas forward.

Once you've grounded the vision, begin to explore the other rings of the Harrington Well-Being Model. Start with some of these and see where the conversation goes.

- **WHO** → Who are we serving? Whose voices need to be heard? What do they need in order to thrive?

- **WHAT** → What aspects of well-being matter most here? How do they connect to our goals?

- **WHEN** → Where are we focused along the continuum of care: upstream prevention, midstream support, or downstream services?

- **HOW** → What systems, structures, and relationships influence daily behavior and experience?

To spark richer dialogue, ask questions like these.

- How do we promote well-being in ways that feel authentic and not performative?

- How do we ensure our everyday actions reflect extraordinary care?

- Where are we unintentionally creating barriers to thriving?

As you talk, incorporate visuals, quotes, and stories from your SWOT analysis—highlighting strengths to build on, weaknesses to improve, opportunities to pursue, and threats to manage. Remember, a SWOT analysis isn't just a list; it's a lens for spotting patterns, identifying areas for growth, and revealing recurring pain points. Share visuals, quotes, stories, and themes from your SWOT. Start developing a common language and shared ownership.

Once your coalition is active and energized, move toward action planning with a tool like the Kellogg Logic Model.[54] This framework helps make priorities visible and connects everyday actions to long-term impact.

- **Inputs:** People, funding, time, partnerships, and infrastructure
- **Activities:** Programs, policies, communications, and training
- **Outputs:** Participation rates, engagement metrics, reach across audiences
- **Outcomes:** Changes in knowledge, behavior, systems, and culture

Mapping these elements together ensures your strategy is both intentional and transparent, and it allows everyone to see how their work contributes to the bigger picture.

Ultimately, well-being is about the lived experience, shifting from transactional to transformative. Anyone can provide coffee; a great coffee shop creates community. Any airline can sell a seat; the difference lies in how people feel during the experience of flying. Your team's role is to turn ordinary interactions into moments of care and connection. When people feel seen, supported, and safe, they flourish. When teams feel trusted, they thrive. And when organizations integrate well-being into everyday life, everyone benefits.

Make It Yours! Make It Happen!

A culture of well-being is created by people, and maintained through shared purpose. Your role isn't to do everything alone, but to connect, empower, and spark momentum. It is time to put your ideas into action.

Reflection

1. Who are three people you could engage, such as an ally, an unexpected connection, and a thoughtful skeptic?

2. What language, values, or themes emerged when you listened to their views on well-being?

3. Which puzzle pieces are already connected? Which are waiting to be placed? Which are still in the box?

Build Your Team

1. Choose one relationship you reflected on and plan a specific outreach step. Start with a conversation, a coffee, or a meeting invitation.

2. Use your Harrington Well-Being Model as a conversation starter to show how their role connects to the bigger picture.

3. Commit to a follow-up action—whether sharing notes, bringing them into a coalition, or aligning their strengths to your WHY.

Every conversation is a spark. Each puzzle piece you place helps reveal the bigger picture: a connected, thriving culture where well-being is everyone's job.

CHAPTER 13

Use Strategic Communication to Transform Your Messages into Momentum

A well-designed well-being model is more than a planning tool—it becomes a brand. It tells the story of who you are and what you value. It creates a shared language and a recognizable image that can unify teams across departments and divisions. Just as the Harrington Well-Being Model graphic acts as the visual anchor for this book, your organization's customized well-being model can become the identity for your health-promoting system, unifying communications, sparking conversation, and enhancing recognition.

When implemented effectively, the model becomes a vital part of the organization's identity—something that employees, students, leaders, and partners can recognize, relate to, and take pride in. You can personalize your model to match your school or organization's colors, logo, or mission statement. Some organizations have added their action words or core values around each ring, while others have adjusted the layout to fit a gear shape, a star, or a flower. Whether laminated on cards, displayed on banners, animated in digital onboarding, or even placed on adhesive bandages handed out by the health center, the model's usefulness increases when it is visible and familiar.

Real-World Examples

- **Bright Orange Pride:** Oklahoma State University, known for its "America's Brightest Orange" brand, designed its wellness model using distinctive orange shades. It instantly conveyed their culture, not just a standard well-being model. They also designed rotating ring models as business cards, held together by a metal brad, with contact details on the back. These memorable tools were used in onboarding, leadership development, and even a TEDx presentation.

- **Tech & Gears:** At the Georgia Institute of Technology, or Georgia Tech, the model was redesigned with mechanical gears, symbolizing the engineering approach and system connectivity.

- **Language Integration:** University of Houston incorporated its five action words—doing, caring, being, connecting, learning—to align communication, branding, and programming. These words appeared in orientation materials, web pages, signage, and presentations, all tied to the "Be Well to Do Well" mission.

When your model appears regularly, it becomes a cultural touchstone. People start to speak its language. It becomes a part of how they think, talk, and plan.

- "That's an upstream intervention."
- "This aligns with emotional well-being."
- "Let's engage both our employee and student audiences."

The true strength of your model lies in its ability to influence everyday actions. One of the most effective ways to do this is by incorporating it into your communication strategy across both internal and external platforms, including email, social media, digital signage, meeting language, and even how you frame your events and materials. When people see themselves and their work reflected in the model, it becomes more than just a diagram—it turns into a mirror of the culture you're building.

> Strategic communication brings your well-being model to life—connecting people to purpose, turning intention into action, and making well-being a visible, natural part of daily culture, not just something discussed when a new program launches.

Communication is not an afterthought; it's a strategy. It's one of the most essential yet often underused tools for building a health-promoting organization. In any systems-level culture shift—like embedding well-being into the fabric of your organization—a coordinated, intentional communication plan transforms good ideas into lasting impact. You don't just need alignment; you need amplification. Communication builds awareness, fosters clarity, and ensures consistency. It's often the missing link between inspiring ideas and real, sustained change.

Message Amplification Through the Rings

How you communicate your well-being model is just the beginning. From there, it becomes an impactful guide for how you speak, brand, and coordinate your efforts across your organization or community. When communication is intentional, well-being is no longer just a program; it becomes a way of life. It infuses every message—whether a campaign, program title, email, or casual conversation—with your organization's core values and strategic direction. By using the five rings of your model as both a strategic filter and a communication lens, you ensure that each message is clear, consistent, and aligned with your broader goals. Whether you're leading change in a business, university, or community, this approach provides coherence, visibility, and impact.

A simple starting point to begin utilizing the five rings in crafting your messaging is to ask yourself these questions:

- **WHY → Purpose:** Does this message reflect our WHY? Is it grounded in the values that matter most to our organization or community?

    Example: "Because your well-being matters—to you, your team, and the people we serve."

- **WHO → Audience:** Who are we trying to reach? Are we speaking their language? Are we taking care to tailor messages for specific groups, such as employees, students, leaders, caregivers, volunteers, and others?

  Example: "Hey, team leads—here's how to support your people during high-stress periods."

- **WHAT → Focus Area:** Which dimension of well-being does this message support? Is it physical, emotional, spiritual, social, or professional (or a combination of two or more)?

  Example: "Let's talk about physical wellness. Have you found the new walking path?"

- **HOW → Strategy Level:** At what level are we influencing change? And are we seeing it through all aspects of the socio-ecological lens, including individual, interpersonal, organizational, environmental, and policy levels?

  Example: "This month, we're focusing on team-based support, starting with how we open meetings."

- **WHEN → Timing / Continuum:** Where does this fall on the continuum of care? What timing are we aiming for (promotion, prevention, early intervention, harm reduction, crisis response, or recovery)?

  Example: "Let's focus on rest and recharge, before the busy season hits."

Speaking of messaging, here's an important note about how you use language. For many years, wellness communication often focused on problems—what was wrong instead of what was strong.

We emphasized risk, not resilience. For example, fear-based messaging about tobacco use had only limited success over time. But rephrasing the conversation around "clean air" made it more inclusive and empowering.

Whenever possible, choose a positive frame. For instance, "Are you stressed?" emphasizes a focus on problems. Asking "Do you feel supported?" encourages connection and possibility. This shift—from pathogenic (problem-focused) to salutogenic (health-generating)—promotes action based on strength and hope. Small language changes can make a big difference. Here are a few additional tips.

- Replace "should" with "could" to lessen guilt and highlight choice.
- Use "and" instead of "but" to encourage collaborative thinking.
- Speak with curiosity, not with judgment.
- Communicate with care and an open mind.

Bottom line? Your model is more than just a framework; it's your message. And clear, strategic, and inclusive communication is how you make it resonate.

Now let's look at a few specific initiatives that can help bring your communications strategy to life. And remember, these are simply strategies that have worked for me—please adapt and tailor them to fit your organization's unique needs.

Build a Concierge-Style Well-Being Hub

Your people shouldn't have to search endlessly for help or to find ways to support their health. A well-designed, concierge-style website—your one-stop hub for well-being—can be one of the most effective tools for integrating this concept into the daily culture of your workplace, campus, or community. Think of it as your digital front porch: welcoming, easy to use, and aligned with your core values. Whether you serve employees, students, or neighbors, the hub can provide both preventive and reactive resources, offering everyday support and urgent assistance in one simple, easy-to-navigate location. To help ensure seamless integration, partner with your marketing or IT team early on to secure their buy-in and expertise.

Whether you're building the online presence yourself or coordinating with a marketing department or resource, here are some strategies to optimize your hub.

Start with what matters most.

At the very top of your home page, include two clear and distinct access points: one for immediate needs and one for everyday support. This dual approach not only helps people in crisis but also shifts your culture toward prevention and proactive care. The first section, which you could name something like Get Help Now, should be bold, highly visible, and easy to find. It should link directly to emergency resources, such as 24/7 crisis or mental health services, campus or workplace safety and security, immediate medical help, and tools for reporting misconduct or safety concerns.

Right beside it, add a second section called something like Support Your Well-Being to highlight everyday tools that help people thrive. Include links to preventive health screenings, physical activity and nutrition resources, mindfulness practices, financial wellness tools, and professional or academic development programs. Also consider adding support for connection and belonging, parenting and caregiving, navigating life transitions, hobby and employee resource groups, and any other supports your organization currently offers. This side-by-side layout demonstrates that your organization supports both urgent and ongoing needs.

Organize by human needs, not departments.

Structure your content around what people need, not where services happen to "live," like One Mental Health. Use clear, everyday language that resonates with real-life experiences. Instead of organizing resources by department, consider grouping them by your WHAT dimensions—such as emotional, physical, and social well-being—or by intuitive categories like mental and emotional health, physical vitality, connection and belonging, academic or career development, financial wellness, spiritual or values-based living, parenting and caregiving, housing and transportation, and crisis support or advocacy.

Infuse each section with your organization's WHY to strengthen a sense of purpose, and label resources by WHO they serve and HOW they contribute to well-being. Ensure that you reflect the full WHEN continuum—from proactive promotion and prevention to timely intervention and long-term recovery. You can also include life-stage or situational pathways like "I'm returning to work," "I'm grieving a loss," or "I'm supporting someone else."

These thoughtful entry points help people quickly find what they need—and demonstrate that your organization genuinely sees and supports the whole person, wherever they are in their journey.

If you serve multiple groups—such as students, employees, or managers—consider creating distinct entry points that directly address their roles and needs. Phrases like "I'm a new employee," "I'm a student," "I manage a team," or "I'm navigating a life change" make the experience more personal and relevant. Each page can showcase tailored resources while still linking back to your main hub. This thoughtful customization helps users feel seen and supported.

Make it the anchor of your strategy.

Your hub can be more than just a web page; it can serve as the core of your well-being strategy. Use it to strengthen your well-being model and initiatives, promote upcoming campaigns and events, share tool kits and trainings, and highlight success stories and testimonials. It can also feature interactive tools, such as quick polls and real-time feedback forms, and engagement opportunities like volunteer sign-ups or grant applications. Ensure every communication—whether it's a flyer, email, newsletter, or presentation—links back to this site. The more it's used, the more people will trust it. Over time, it will become the primary space for support, resources, and inspiration.

Support long-term sustainability.

A well-being hub can also help your organization achieve its growth and sustainability goals. Include features like a Text to

Give link or donation portal to support new initiatives. Provide opportunities for peer support or volunteer engagement. Create cobranded pages with community partners or nonprofits. Add a Get Involved section to help recruit new Well-Being Activators or team champions. These elements expand the hub's impact and foster community ownership. When your hub reflects your well-being framework in both content and tone, it becomes more than just a directory—it transforms into a dynamic representation of your organization's commitment to care.

Activate a Network of Well-Being Champions

Well-being doesn't grow on good ideas alone; it grows through people. One of your most powerful tools and a best practice for driving cultural change is a network of what I call Well-Being Activators, often referred to as Wellness Ambassadors, Champions, Influencers, or Integrators. I prefer the term Well-Being Activators because it conveys energy, agency, and action. These individuals aren't just messengers; they're culture carriers. They bring your strategy to life where it matters most: on the ground and in meetings, break rooms, and everyday interactions.

In many ways, Well-Being Activators resemble public health community health workers (CHWs) and promotoras, because they provide culturally grounded health education navigation and advocacy; and more importantly, come from the communities and departments they serve. Most are not licensed professionals; however, unlike CHWs or promotoras, Well-Being Activators are usually volunteers. With each, their role is relational and cultural rather than clinical, and their impact relies on building trust and fostering genuine conversations within the everyday life of organizations. Well-Being Activators take this further by fostering trust, sparking meaningful conversations, and making well-being authentic and relevant within teams. They bridge the gap between organizational vision and daily actions, ensuring that well-being is not just a program but also a shared way of working and living.

Well-being champions are also highlighted as a criterion in the free HERO (Health Enhancement Research Organization) Scorecard—one of the most widely used benchmarking tools for evaluating workplace health and well-being programs. The scorecard examines organizational practices across key areas, such as leadership support, program design, engagement, measurement, and alignment with business goals.[55]

Here are the core attributes of a strong Activator program.

Choose people who help you convey and amplify your messages.

A Well-Being Activator isn't someone in a professional role, such as a peer educator, health coach, or program staff member. Their role is relational and cultural. Over time, they become trusted voices and valuable sources of insight, and they bring myriad benefits to your organization, including the following:

- Incorporating well-being into daily team culture
- Enhancing the saturation, visibility, and consistency of messages
- Establishing bidirectional communication: exchanging messages outward and receiving feedback inward
- Enabling cross-team collaboration and peer learning

- Fostering grassroots energy while aligning with system-level goals

Make the program accessible and supportive.

To ensure your network of Well-Being Activators is both effective and sustainable, design the program to be simple yet impactful—an approach widely recognized as a best practice in employee health. Participation should be voluntary but supported by managers. Requiring approval from supervisors helps legitimize the role, secures protected time to attend monthly meetings, and encourages team leaders to allow Activators to share content during department gatherings. This structure reinforces the value of the role while integrating it into the workplace routines.

A quick note on middle managers: They are often overlooked and overworked, yet they hold significant power to influence culture. When engaged and supported, they can become true well-being multipliers—equipping, inspiring, and amplifying across teams.

Start with an engaging and energizing orientation session that introduces your well-being model, clarifies expectations, shares well-being resources, and fosters connection among participants. Offer training opportunities like Mental Health First Aid and QPR (Question, Persuade, and Refer) or other supportive resources.

Consistent engagement is crucial for active participation; brief monthly huddles or virtual check-ins can offer opportunities to share successes, highlight upcoming campaigns, and maintain momentum.

Branded recognition boosts pride and awareness. Small but meaningful items—like pins, lanyards, stickers, or digital badges—not only celebrate participation but also encourage a sense of identity and community within the network.

Finally, create simple feedback loops by encouraging Activators to gather informal input from their teams. Quick check-in questions like "What's your biggest well-being challenge right now?" or "What helps your team feel most connected?" offer valuable insights that can shape future strategies. These everyday interactions build a culture of listening, responsiveness, and continuous improvement.

Build sustainability into the plan.

To keep your Well-Being Activator community energized and engaged over time, aim to have at least one Activator in each department, functional unit, or student group, ensuring broad and cross-functional representation. This includes key areas, such as HR, academics, operations, facilities, and other relevant departments. Create opportunities for Well-Being Activators to stay connected through private online groups, photo sharing, or story exchanges that foster a sense of community and shared purpose.

For example, Oklahoma State University established a private online space where their Wellness Innovators posted bulletin board photos, shared tips, and reflected on team conversations, resulting in a vibrant, supportive, and idea-rich network.

Celebrating milestones, highlighting success stories, and inviting new ideas can help sustain momentum and strengthen connections. With clear expectations and ongoing support, Activators develop into a strong distributed communication network. They reinforce central messages while customizing them to their specific departmental contexts, model the behaviors you want to see, and lead by example—not through titles, but through actions. When departments are encouraged to co-create and co-own the message, they become co-authors of the culture you're aiming to build.

Monthly Themes: A Cornerstone of Communication Strategy

One of the most effective tools for fostering a well-being culture is a coordinated calendar featuring monthly or quarterly themes. These themes should be driven by your WHY and WHO, not simply by popular observances such as Breast Cancer Awareness Month or Mental Health Awareness Month, unless those topics directly support your strategic focus. Too often, the calendar dictates the message, rather than the other way around.

For example, when I first began as AVP, my wellness director was short-staffed and had just been tasked with starting a campus food pantry to meet growing demand. At the same time, he felt overwhelmed preparing the extensive annual HIV/AIDS program based on the national monthly topic. Curious, I asked about the WHY and the WHO.

"Is there a significant unmet need for HIV/AIDS support on our campus?"

He shared that there wasn't, but explained, "We've always done it. People expect it."

I suggested we redirect our focus to food and nutrition, aligning programming and messaging with the current documented needs of our students. He agreed, and together we built a strong nutrition communication strategy that was really well received. This shift not only met people where they were but also demonstrated how intentional alignment can amplify its impact.

These themes unify messaging, synchronize efforts across teams or departments, and make well-being visible, relevant, and actionable. They establish a rhythm and foster a sense of familiarity. Aligned themes also reduce program duplication, generate momentum, and help individuals see how their efforts connect to a larger purpose. Over time, this consistency builds trust and promotes a shared culture of care, while still allowing room for creativity and local adaptation.

Creating a meaningful annual theme calendar isn't something to do alone. The most effective, and enjoyable, calendars are made through collaboration. Gather diverse voices from across the organization—such as wellness committees, communications teams, HR, and operational units—and invite them to help identify the key moments, opportunities, and rhythms that matter most. These discussions often generate valuable insights and build a sense of shared ownership.

I'll never forget a particular calendar planning discussion where a leader's eyes lit up with enthusiasm. She had been working on a major event. After reviewing the broader calendar, she eagerly adjusted its timing a few months later to match the newly identified month on Sustainability and Personal Energy. That's true integration—when individual efforts align with collective priorities to create something stronger together, without adding extra work.

Here are a few tips to help you establish a year of theme-driven communications strategy.

Align themes with natural rhythms.

Your organization or community likely follows a familiar rhythm, marked by seasonal shifts, fiscal years, academic schedules, or signature events. Connecting your well-being themes to these natural cycles makes them more relevant, timely, and engaging. When a message aligns with what is already happening, it feels less like "one more thing" and more like part of daily life.

It can also extend beyond your organization. For example, during the Olympics, your team might highlight increased physical activity or teamwork. If a major arts festival is happening nearby, the theme could focus on creativity, trying a new hobby, or celebrating cultural expression. By anchoring well-being initiatives to existing rhythms, you amplify impact and make the work feel more organic and integrated.

You can also rotate through your organization's core well-being dimensions or model rings. Here are some examples.

- January might focus on being, encouraging reflection, and renewal.
- February could emphasize connecting, with themes like belonging and kindness.
- April might combine Moving & Meaning, pairing physical activity with sustainability.
- You could do Welcome & Belonging in August, aligning with the start of a school or fiscal year.
- Try Courage & Growth in October, framed as a "do something scary" month.

Don't hesitate to blend dimensions as needed. For instance, a February theme like Caring for Yourself and Others can integrate emotional and social wellness, while April's Move Your Body, Recharge Your Mind could merge physical and spiritual aspects. Naming the themes is a creative and energizing step in the process. Invite playful, meaningful, or poetic phrasing that reflects your culture. These aren't just slogans; they serve as strategic anchors to support your mission and engage your people.

Include attention-grabbing elements.

Once themes are selected, it's time to bring them to life. Each monthly campaign should focus on a few engaging aspects. Start with a simple *gee whiz* fact—something surprising or memorable, like "Employees who take short daily walks report 23% less stress." Follow it with a clear, realistic *call to action* that people can try immediately, such as "Try a 10-minute reset—walk, breathe, or stretch." Then gather a few *relevant resources*: a walking group map, HR benefits, a mindfulness guide—whatever best supports that month's message. Ideally, these messages are measurable; however, even raising awareness and establishing consistency across departments represents a significant cultural shift.

Make it accessible and actionable.

Once your calendar and content are ready, it's time to intentionally roll them out across your organization. Visibility, consistency, and repetition are key. A multi-modal communication plan ensures your messages are seen, heard, and remembered, without becoming overwhelming.

Start by designing a branded visual asset for each theme. This could be a poster or graphic that features your fact, a brief call to action, and a QR code linking to the resources on your central well-being hub. Distribute these tool kits widely to Well-Being Activators, department leaders, and team leads so they can display them in break rooms, share via email, or present at team meetings. Ready-to-use materials make it easier for Well-Being Activators and others to incorporate the theme into their local culture.

Coordinate messaging across various platforms, including newsletters, social media, digital signage, intranet portals, meeting slides, and event announcements. To simplify this, provide each team with a ready-to-use tool kit containing sample posts, talking points, email templates, and quick ideas on how to engage colleagues.

Most importantly, encourage teams to customize the theme with their voice and examples. One size doesn't fit all. For instance, during a financial well-being theme, HR might focus on retirement planning, while student services promote budgeting apps or scholarship info. These differences make the message more meaningful and relatable to diverse audiences, without diluting the core message. When each department shares a common theme authentically, well-being becomes an integral part of your organization's culture, not just another campaign.

You don't need to build everything from scratch. Many effective communication strategies improve existing practices. Integrate your well-being messages into your organization's regular routines, such as team meetings, staff newsletters, onboarding, welcome events, or annual retreats. Whether it's a town hall update or compliance training, these are all chances to naturally include a well-being perspective.

Use a mix of touchpoints, including internal and external social media, hallway monitors, HR or student portals, lobby posters, slide decks, and even word of mouth from champions and Well-Being Activators. The more places people see and hear your message, the more likely it is to stick. Traditional marketing suggests the Rule of Seven—people need to hear a message at least seven times before they take action or remember it. When well-being is consistently woven into familiar systems, it becomes a core part of how your organization communicates, connects, and leads.

Design for storytelling.

Data is powerful, but stories are memorable. Encourage people to share examples of how they're "living the model" in small, meaningful ways. Maybe someone leads stretch breaks before meetings, another manager consistently demonstrates vulnerability and trust, or a colleague creates a gratitude board in the break room. These simple actions bring your well-being strategy to life and show others how they can contribute too.

Highlight these stories in internal newsletters, on digital signage, on social media, or even at town halls. Storytelling humanizes your strategy and showcases everyday champions—people who are already fostering a culture of care and connection without formal titles. When others see these examples, they're often inspired to follow.

Certified Healthy Program: A Tool for Awareness, Alignment, and Action

The Certified Healthy program is a cost-effective, impactful initiative that encourages departments or units to evaluate their well-being efforts and earn a designation, such as Striving to be Certified, Certified, or Certified Gold. More than just a badge of honor, this program serves as a catalyst for self-reflection, the deeper integration of well-being into daily operations, and the celebration of progress.[56] It is an excellent tool for the Well-Being Activator and middle managers. Additionally, this integrated approach enhances awareness of what a health-promoting organization looks like, shares current efforts and opportunities, encourages friendly competition, and highlights informal leaders and early adopters. It aligns with your organizational well-being goals and offers a practical way to understand your current culture of care. While also providing well-being data, departments learn from each other, and the entire community benefits from a shared sense of momentum and purpose.

Here are some tips on how to ensure your Certified Healthy program is impactful.

Go beyond simple recognition.

A thoughtfully designed tool does more than just provide acknowledgment. It encourages dialogue, highlights strengths, and empowers internal champions, while gathering data on the organization's well-being. This optional tool should feature a checklist of well-being actions that reflect multiple dimensions and address both upstream (preventive) and downstream (responsive) strategies. Consider organizing the checklist with two levels of criteria:

required items that meet baseline organizational expectations and optional items that raise awareness and contribute to a flexible point system. Supervisor signatures are vital for approval and buy-in.

At one organization, a middle manager initially declined to sign, humbly noting that her team was "only striving." But by the following year, their commitment and progress led them to achieve Certified Gold status. This change shows the power of structured reflection and the motivation that comes from seeing a clear path toward improvement.

A couple of open-ended questions at the end of the survey, such as "How is your department currently thriving?" and "What are your biggest well-being challenges?" help generate meaningful insights and data. Create space for departments to identify their current priorities and obstacles—this feedback can shape broader strategy and customized support. This assessment can also serve as an internal alignment tool, aiding departments to reflect, reengage, and develop within your overall well-being strategy.

Use a tiered strategy to encourage participation.

Offer multiple levels of recognition to promote inclusivity and motivate continued progress.

- The Striving level recognizes departments just starting their well-being journey and increasing awareness.

- The Certified level acknowledges those who meet established criteria and align with organizational goals.

- The Certified Gold designation honors departments that go above and beyond, serving as inspiring models for others.

Recognition can take many meaningful forms, such as a digital badge, certificate, window cling, or even an icon for email signatures. Present awards with visible appreciation—a handwritten note, an announcement from a senior leader, or a personal visit from a wellness champion. These simple but powerful gestures inspire pride, spark new ideas, and demonstrate that well-being is genuinely valued throughout the organization.

Add mini-grants for extra engagement.

To promote creativity and participation, pair the Certified Healthy program with small mini-grants (such as $100). Invite departments to apply by answering a single reflective question: "If awarded this grant, how would you improve well-being in your department?" This simple approach encourages grassroots innovation and ownership. It helps you assess readiness and identify resource gaps, often generating momentum, even among teams that aren't selected—many go on to implement their ideas anyway.

Make it ongoing and actionable.

To sustain the impact, keep the application process open throughout the year to increase awareness while providing recognition annually. Offer a support guide with examples, ideas, and simple how-tos to help departments take action. Celebrate certified teams regularly—monthly or quarterly—by highlighting their stories, wins, and lessons learned. Over time, observe themes and trends across departments to inform your system-wide strategy.

The more visible and embedded the Certified Healthy program becomes, the more it fosters a culture of well-being, shared accountability, and continuous improvement, making it one of the most valuable tools in your organizational well-being tool kit.

Hire a health communication specialist.

If your team has room to grow, one of the best early hires you can make is a health communication specialist. They can ensure consistency, creativity, and connection and are trained in health communication. They act as a translator, bridging the gap between public health, marketing, and organizational culture. They also help navigate the nuances of language across disciplines. For example, in developing national standards for safe patient handling, we added the term *mobility* to shift focus from passive care to empowering patients. But physical therapists initially resisted—because for them, mobility had a different clinical meaning. After a shared conversation, we aligned on the intention and moved forward. That's the power of dialogue.

Start small and keep the WHY in sight.

You don't need to do everything at once, and in fact, you can't. Cultural transformation occurs through steady, coordinated, and courageous steps. That's why it's crucial to begin with small, strategic wins that build credibility and momentum. These could include launching your first monthly well-being theme, adding a shared well-being slide to all presentations, forming a cross-functional wellness council, piloting a Certified Healthy recognition program, or hosting a retreat to align existing efforts with your model. These are more than tasks; they are signals to your organization that well-being is important, that it's everyone's responsibility, and that alignment is both achievable and impactful. As you focus on these initial steps, don't lose sight of your larger purpose. Keep your long-term vision clearly in focus. Whether your goal is to become a recognized health-promoting organization, improve population-level mental health, or eliminate preventable burnout, these ambitious objectives help unify and guide each small step forward.

Make it Yours! Make It Happen!

Every message has power. With intention and alignment, your communications can shift from one-off announcements to ongoing signals that well-being is everyone's responsibility—and everyone's opportunity.

Reflection

1. What communication tools are already in place? Are they being used effectively?

2. What one message does your population most need to hear right now?

3. Who could be your first Well-Being Activator? What monthly theme would resonate most next month?

Turn Your Messages into Momentum

1. Choose one reflection insight and design a small communication-driven strategy around it.

2. Implement it within the next two weeks—whether that's a theme launch, a message campaign, or activating a champion.

3. Use your Harrington Well-Being Model as a visual anchor to tie the message back to purpose and culture.

CHAPTER 14

Tell Your Story with Data to Strengthen Your Insight, Alignment, and Impact

At an Air Force base in the early 2000s, the Health and Wellness Center had become overlooked, almost like just another box to check. Their report at the hospital commander's monthly meeting consisted of a single slide on tobacco cessation class attendance, when the other departments and units had extensive and expansive reporting dashboards. However, when they added simple pre- and post-program evaluation dashboards—along with tobacco use by squadron determined by dental records, and tobacco use rates and trends compared to national and healthy people data—they told a more compelling story. Commanders took notice. Programs expanded. The center gained visibility and funding, and with the support of the commander, they became the first tobacco-free Air Force medical group and fitness center. Measurement shifted the narrative and the outcome.

In a hospital intensive-care unit, a leaking ceiling kept a room offline for weeks. Repeated maintenance requests were ignored—until the nurse rephrased the issue: "This bed is losing us $5,000 a day." The ceiling was fixed the next morning.

When data appeals to something your audience values, such as money, safety, or efficiency, it becomes persuasive.

When a community pediatrician raised concerns about childhood obesity, the solution wasn't a diet plan. It was a family and community-focused wellness program emphasizing food literacy and joyful movement. Data showed increases in shared meals, more outdoor activities, and even menu changes in local childcare centers. The shift was systemic and measurable in significant ways.

As you may have guessed, these are all real-life examples I've been part of over the years. I'm not a data scientist, but I do get excited about measurement and using it to tell a story. I agree that terms like *data*, *measurement*, and *evaluation* may sometimes feel intimidating or dull. But what if we viewed measurement differently? What if, instead of seeing it as just an obligation, we saw it as a tool for clarity, influence, and inspiration—something that helps tell a compelling story? That's when it gets thrilling!

Like the Air Force commander, identify what matters to your audience, share the right evidence, and meet their WIIFM. In his case, it was about becoming the first tobacco-free base. With our data, we secured his support to make it a reality. Think about your C-suite and senior leaders: What data would help them advocate for—and fund—your organizational health and well-being?

The good news is you don't have to be a data scientist to use measurement as a storytelling tool to improve your work, showcase impact, and champion what matters most. All you need is purpose, curiosity, and a willingness to connect data with your values. When approached with empathy and strategy, measurement becomes a powerful method to build credibility, fuel improvement, and drive change.

> Strategic measurement helps you tell the story of what's working, what's possible, and where to go next—creating common language for progress and collaboration, and affirming that well-being is worth investing in.

The Challenge: Measuring the Intangible and Complex

Unlike clinical metrics such as blood pressure or cholesterol, well-being is a complex and deeply human concept. It's about connection, purpose, culture, and community. It's about what you prevent as much as what you provide. And it's often hard to quantify.

The challenge isn't just that these outcomes are intangible; it's also that well-being work is inherently multidimensional and multilayered. Most efforts don't operate in a single lane—they span across departments, address multiple levels of the Socio-Ecological Model, and cover numerous dimensions of well-being. That's the strength of a whole-system approach, but it also makes it harder to identify cause and effect. Unlike a clinical trial, which controls variables and measures a specific input, well-being initiatives often involve many simultaneous influences. You might introduce a new training, improve a workspace, and launch a recognition program all at once. When a change occurs, it isn't easy to attribute it to a single action. But this complexity indicates a mature, integrated effort—not a flaw.

That's why traditional ROI doesn't tell the whole story, even though showing the "shift to the left" and cost savings is compelling and remains important. While it measures financial savings and risk reduction, it rarely captures the broader ripple effects of well-being—like joy, trust, engagement, or organizational reputation. That's where value on investment comes in. VOI emphasizes what people value and experience: a deeper sense of belonging, improved morale, stronger relationships, and increased equity. It's less transactional, more transformational, and often more aligned with your mission.

Duplication to Clarity

In many organizations—whether universities, businesses, or community agencies—important data is often collected by different departments or teams working toward a common goal. At one university, we found that data on sexual violence was tracked separately by four different departments—public safety, student affairs, counseling services, and the Title IX office. Each department had good intentions and valid reasons for collecting data, but because their efforts weren't coordinated, there was a confusing lack of clarity. And their efforts occurred in silos, with no shared system for coordination.

As we started asking questions—who's collecting what, where is it stored, and why—we discovered overlapping data sources and gaps we hadn't noticed before. Were we double-counting? Were key trends being missed? Without a unified approach, we couldn't be certain. We gathered key stakeholders to map the landscape, identifying what was being tracked, the definitions being used, and where opportunities for alignment existed. This collaboration resulted in a centralized tracking tool that honored each team's specific needs and confidentiality requirements while removing unnecessary duplication.

The outcome was more than just streamlined data; it brought greater clarity, enhanced collaboration, and enabled better-informed decisions. By working across silos, we transformed fragmented data into a stronger narrative and set ourselves up to respond with more focus, coordination, and impact.

Making Data Meaningful

To go beyond attendance and satisfaction surveys, it's helpful to understand how different types of data relate along a spectrum.

- **Inputs** indicate what you invested, such as time, staffing, partnerships, or funds.

- **Outputs** document what was achieved, such as events held, policies implemented, or the number of participants reached.

- **Outcomes** describe the short-term changes, such as knowledge gained, behaviors influenced, or new attitudes observed.

- **Impact** highlights long-term changes, such as improvements in health outcomes, systems, equity, or culture.

Your logic model can be especially useful for leveraging data, particularly when developing grant proposals or strategic plans, since it employs terms and structures commonly recognized in these areas.

Another effective data collection tool is the Certified Healthy program. This approach provides annual data that can be used to evaluate efforts, reflect on organizational culture, and celebrate achievements. Certified Healthy assessments are structured self-evaluations that enable departments or units to assess their practices across key areas, including leadership alignment, physical and social environments, inclusiveness, and programming. Even without external validation, completing a Certified Healthy assessment promotes honest dialogue, uncovers blind spots, and aligns local initiatives with broader organizational goals.

Whether formal or informal, these frameworks provide insight into understanding the chain reaction from effort to impact.

Additionally, to make your data meaningful, it must connect with the people you're trying to reach. Whether you're in a business, a university, or a community organization, each stakeholder has unique priorities, and your job is to link your efforts to what matters most to them. A university provost might focus on student retention and success. A business leader may be concerned about employee performance, brand reputation, or client satisfaction. A city council member might be driven by public trust, resource efficiency, or community well-being. Even within the same organization, different departments or decision-makers will view things through different lenses.

To align effectively, ask these questions:

- What is most important to them?
- What questions are they already asking?
- What types of data or insights would enable them to act?

Well-being often intersects with broader strategic goals, including employee engagement, student success, operational efficiency, innovation, and public health. The correct data, clearly presented and thoughtfully shared, can refine those goals and demonstrate how your efforts contribute to collective success. Ultimately, this isn't about just telling your story; it's about connecting the dots. Data becomes most impactful when it speaks the language of those involved, helping them see how your work supports what they already value.

Designing for Measurement from Start to Finish

The most effective measurement starts before the program begins, not after it's already in motion. Whether you're launching a well-being ambassador initiative, a new training series, or a culture-building campaign, don't wait until the end to figure out how to measure success. Instead, begin by defining your desired outcomes. What are you trying to change or improve? What is your

WHY? It could be increased peer support, better cross-department collaboration, or a shift in how leaders visibly promote well-being. Be clear about what success looks like, and then work backward to achieve it.

Ask yourself early on…

- How will we know this is happening?
- What kinds of stories, behaviors, or data will show progress?
- What does impact look like in real life, not just on paper?

From there, include simple yet intentional evaluation touchpoints, such as quick check-ins, reflective journaling, informal observations, or brief surveys. These don't have to be complex. In fact, the most effective evaluation practices are often those that feel natural and are easy to maintain.

When you embed measurement from the start, it becomes part of the program's rhythm. Instead of feeling like an extra chore, it acts as a compass, gently guiding your work toward greater clarity, learning, and impact.

Then once the program is off and running, be sure to go beyond the sign-in sheet. Attendance may indicate the number of people who attended, but it doesn't reveal whether the program was effective or meaningful, or if it made a difference. Numbers alone can't answer questions like: Did participants leave more informed? More inspired? More ready to act? To truly evaluate impact, ask deeper questions: What do we want participants to think, feel, or do differently? And how will we know if that happens?

One practical method is to use short, targeted post-event surveys. These typically capture essential data, such as participant satisfaction and how attendees learned about the event. Adding a few questions about knowledge gained, linked to the learning outcomes, and the intent to apply what was learned can uncover a much deeper and more meaningful story. When paired with the same assessment conducted before the event, the comparison highlights real change. These micro-metrics may seem modest on their own, but collectively they provide real-time insights that guide smarter decisions and fuel continuous improvement.

It's also essential to disaggregate your data—analyzing who participated and who didn't. Are there consistent gaps by role, demographic, or department? What might that reveal about access, inclusion, or interest? Like the swimming lessons, disaggregation helps identify blind spots, highlight equity issues, and ensure that your programs reach and resonate with the audiences who need them most.

In short, effective evaluation isn't about gathering more data; it's about gathering the *right* data to improve outcomes, demonstrate value, and increase your impact.

Creative and Collaborative Measurement to Quantify Impact

Some of the most vital elements of a successful organization—trust, belonging, inclusion, and joy—are also the hardest to measure. Yet these cultural signs are essential for well-being. Just because they're difficult to quantify doesn't mean they're impossible or unworthy of measurement.

Tools like the PERMA-Profiler, HERO Scorecard, Flourishing Scale, Gallup Well-Being Index, and CDC Worksite Health Scorecard provide structured methods for reflecting on cultural health. Although these tools differ in scope and complexity, they provide easy ways to evaluate aspects such as meaning, engagement, and workplace climate. At the same time, a well-designed homegrown survey can be valuable, capturing insights about organizational culture, individual wellness, awareness of resources, and perceived needs. Together, these tools help paint a more complete picture of both strengths and opportunities.

That said, measurement doesn't need to be formal to be meaningful. At Georgia Tech, we introduced a Kindness Coins initiative in collaboration with a colleague from the Business School Servant Leadership program, following repeated concerns about a lack of connection on campus. When students witnessed acts of compassion, they were given coins to pass along, each one trackable online. We collected stories and shared them broadly, providing a qualitative sense of campus kindness—and fostering a culture of noticing that people could see and feel.

At Oklahoma State University, I collaborated with the facilities team and a colleague who shared my enthusiasm for innovative wellness projects to create Pete's Discovery Tour—a geocaching challenge that combined physical activity with wellness themes. She designed the concept and selected the locations to include on the route. I developed the wellness touchpoints, managed the messaging, and tracked participation. The program attracted students, staff, visiting families, and alumni who brought their grandchildren. Although it wasn't a conventional health intervention, it enhanced both physical and social well-being; provided valuable data on engagement, activity, and community bonding; and also served as a marketing tool for the university's advancement division. The insights we gained reinforced the case for expanding experiential wellness programs.

At times, my role was less about creating new ways to determine outcomes and more about improving processes. At one university, survey fatigue was so high that responses had stopped entirely. I facilitated a cross-department discussion and discovered how many overlapping surveys were being sent from different units. We established a shared assessment calendar to coordinate timing, minimize redundancy, and focus on the most meaningful metrics. The outcome: Participation rates increased again, and we rebuilt trust while continuing to collect the necessary data.

In each of these cases, I found that simple, well-designed tracking tools—whether kindness stories, wellness challenges, or coordinated surveys—could provide both formal and informal signals of cultural change. The key was ensuring that every measure connected back to the WHY and offered actionable insights, rather than collecting data for its own sake.

Data can reveal successes that might otherwise go unnoticed, offering a vital first step toward greater visibility and credibility. It can highlight when you've closed a gap, reduced duplication, or shifted strategies upstream toward prevention. Sometimes this is clear in measurable ways—such as increased clinical engagement for early intervention—but often it manifests through patterns, relationships, and cultural shifts that are harder to quantify. You may notice silos dissolving, messaging becoming more consistent, or programs aligning across departments. Conversations move from "Whose lane is this?" to "How can we do this together?" Subtle signals—such as well-being discussed in everyday meetings, shared language across teams, or informal support in communal spaces—are not superficial. There's evidence that systemic transformation is taking root, often sensed in the atmosphere before it appears on any chart.

Remember, measuring culture isn't about perfection—it's about paying attention, noticing what's emerging, and naming what matters. It's also about nurturing the conditions that allow well-being to thrive.

Equity and Experience: Measuring with Empathy

Truly inclusive measurement goes beyond asking "What's happening?" It questions "For who?" Who benefits from your efforts? Who might be overlooked and why? And equally important, how do people experience what you're offering?

Data without context can obscure inequalities and create a misleading sense of progress. That's why empathy-driven approaches—such as interviews, focus groups, and journey mapping—are vital complements to quantitative metrics. These human-centered methods animate the numbers by showcasing lived experiences, not just statistical trends. They highlight where access gaps exist, identify unintentional barriers, and reveal the subtle ways policies and programs are experienced in real life. Most importantly, they offer insights into how your strategies are received by actual people—not just how they appear on a dashboard—ensuring your work is rooted in both evidence and empathy.

Even more powerful is the opportunity for co-designed solutions. When those impacted by policies and programs are involved in the process—shaping questions, interpreting results, and suggesting changes—your efforts become more meaningful and trustworthy. This kind of measurement fosters trust, inclusion, and transparency.

I've seen this firsthand. When launching a university food pantry, we didn't decide what to stock from our office. We collaborated with the food pantry provider and conducted informal focus groups with students, staff, and community partners to determine which foods were most needed, culturally appropriate, and easy to prepare. Their input shaped everything from inventory and pantry hours to communication strategies. The result was higher participation, less waste, and a sense of pride in a resource built *with* the community, not *for* it.

In the tobacco story that opened this chapter, our commander didn't make it happen alone. We didn't just gather data and hand over a report—we sat down with leaders and squadron members, reviewed the results together, and listened to their perspectives. When commanders and service members saw the numbers for themselves, they leaned in, offering ideas and helping shape cessation strategies. The energy shifted. Buy-in grew because the solutions were theirs too. With the advocacy of our commander, that collaboration truly made it happen.

When people see themselves reflected in the process—not just as survey takers but as contributors to the bigger picture—they're more likely to participate, share, and lead. The result is data that not only guides decisions but also builds community.

Measuring with empathy doesn't mean sacrificing rigor. It involves expanding your view to include experience alongside outcomes, context alongside content, and relationships alongside results.

Because equity isn't just a data point; it's a core principle. And by measuring with empathy, we move one step closer to making it a reality.

Recognition as a Data Point

Recognition goes beyond just a pat on the back; it's data with heart. It reflects values in action, signals priorities, and offers visible proof that well-being is taken seriously. Whether it's a national award or local recognition, it can motivate and serve as a meaningful way to measure success. National programs like the Robert Wood Johnson Foundation (RWJF) Culture of Health Prize, Active Minds Healthy Campus Award, Joy in Medicine (AMA), and the Fit-Friendly Worksite (American Heart Association) highlight and honor organizations that incorporate well-being into their culture and operations. These awards and others spotlight excellence, enhance reputation, boost morale, and open doors for external funding or partnership opportunities.

Equally impactful are local or internal recognitions, such as Certified Healthy programs, wellness leader awards, or team-level shoutouts. These provide regular accessible ways to acknowledge progress and foster a culture of appreciation. Even small gestures, like handwritten notes or digital badges, can increase visibility and promote ongoing engagement.

Besides the celebration itself, recognition programs provide concrete, story-rich data. They reveal how departments are leading, where innovation happens, and how culture evolves over time. They can also help set benchmarks, track progress, and pinpoint areas needing extra support.

Tools and Frameworks: Mapping What Matters Across Sectors

Whether you're working to align efforts within your organization or compare with others, having trusted tools that guide, evaluate, and highlight your progress is valuable. Luckily, you're not starting from scratch.

A valuable resource for those seeking to connect data and meaning is the work of Wendy Lynch, PhD.[57] As a researcher and author, Lynch excels at translating complex data into actionable insights that leaders and teams can easily apply. Her focus on human performance, value, and the business case for well-being makes her particularly relevant to organizations trying to connect measurement to impact.

A collection of frameworks and scorecards—created across public health, business, higher education, and global well-being sectors—can support your efforts. These tools serve different roles: Some provide a comprehensive assessment framework, others offer benchmarks for comparison, and some give focused guidance on specific areas like mental health, safety, or equity. When carefully chosen and tailored, they can help you identify gaps, recognize strengths, and align your well-being initiatives with larger priorities.

In the Additional Resources Guide, I have shared a list of tools and frameworks that are not meant to be exhaustive, or necessarily permanent. They're simply the ones that influenced my work—a short starting list I wish I'd had. As political climates, organizational priorities, and societal needs evolve, so will the resources you find most relevant. Think of them as conversation starters, not rigid prescriptions. They're here to spark creativity, broaden your perspective, and help you explore approaches that align with your unique WHY, WHO, and context.

Remember that no single tool does everything—and that's exactly the point. The resources you use aren't about strict compliance or competition; they're about learning, aligning, and refining your strategy. By combining multiple data tools, you can compare your organization's priorities with national or sector trends, see how efforts match across departments or systems, detect overlaps or duplications in reporting, and find credible benchmarks to inform strategic investments. You'll also find that they can support goals like accreditation, recognition, or funding applications.

A practical method is to create a crosswalk (yes, another one) that maps your organization's internal strategies—such as well-being priorities, equity and inclusion objectives, or benefits programs—against one or more external frameworks. Framing these as commitments to fairness, respect, and opportunity keeps the focus on creating environments where all people can thrive, regardless of political climate. This simple visual alignment can reveal both gaps and redundancies, helping you clarify where to deepen impact, streamline data collection, or better tell your story.

At its best, data serves as both a mirror and a megaphone. It reflects where you are, highlights what's working, and points toward what's next. It helps you spot gaps, celebrate successes, and make informed choices—not just for today's programs but also for tomorrow's strategies. Just as importantly, it gives voice to work that might otherwise go unnoticed, amplifying your message, building support, and showing that well-being isn't a side project but a core driver of thriving people, systems, and cultures. And because data builds trust, it fosters transparency and makes your efforts more understandable to those who may not yet fully appreciate the impact. The key is to find it, understand it, and use it—simply and purposefully. Start with what you already have: Explore one metric more deeply, tell one clearer story, or bring one new partner into the conversation. Measurement doesn't have to be perfect; it just has to move you, and others, forward with clarity and confidence.

Make It Yours! Make It Happen!

Every data point is a seed, and every story is the sunlight that helps it grow. Together, they create a living narrative of your culture's well-being journey, building a portfolio that demonstrates outcomes, informs leaders, and strengthens the case for funding. The key is to measure what matters most and share it in ways that resonate with your culture.

Reflection

1. What story do you most want to tell with your well-being efforts?

2. Who do you need to influence or align with? What kind of data or story would resonate with them?

3. Where might you be duplicating efforts or missing gaps? How could you measure more intentionally?

Tell a Story with Data

1. Choose one small story this week that connects data with impact (a program, theme, or culture shift).

2. Share it in a simple format—one slide, a visual, or a short narrative.

3. Note where the data added clarity and where storytelling could have made it stronger.

CHAPTER 15

Tips from My Journey to Help You Thrive, Personally and Professionally

Some of the most valuable lessons I've learned about leadership, resilience, and vision didn't come from a meeting room or a strategic plan—they came from the road, the mountain, and the mission. And if something catches your attention—just do it!

Take Ride the Rockies, a weeklong cycling tour through Colorado's mountains. Hundreds of miles, back-to-back days, and passes climbing thousands of feet into thin air. I was impressed that my friends had taken on this challenge, and when someone told me

"You could too!" I decided to give it a try. On the first morning, as we began the ascent, my legs and lungs both protested. But I learned to break it down: one pedal stroke at a time, one curve at a time. I began to celebrate the milestones—cresting a hill, reaching the next rest stop, finding a steady rhythm. And I learned that the support of others—a shared energy bar, a cheer from a stranger—could carry me farther than I thought possible.

Then there was Mount Kilimanjaro. I reached the summit on Christmas Day, 2017. The climb was about more than just physical endurance; it was about patience, preparation, and adaptability. Weather changes, altitude difficulties, and the mental discipline to keep moving forward at a slow, steady pace ("Pole, pole," pronounced POH-leh, POH-leh, as our guides reminded us, "Slowly, slowly") reflected the long-term process of culture change. The joy at the summit wasn't just in the view—as it was completely clouded in—it was knowing that every step, every adjustment, and every moment of doubt overcome was part of the victory.

Long before those climbs, my Air Force service taught me the importance of mission clarity and team readiness. In the military, success depends on aligning individual strengths with a shared purpose, adapting in real time, and maintaining high morale even under pressure. I learned that preparation is only half the work—trust, communication, and shared resolve are what make the mission possible.

Whether on a mountain pass at 19,000 feet or on a military base, the lessons remain the same: Pace yourself, prepare thoroughly, adapt frequently, and surround yourself with people who share the vision. Building a health-promoting organization is no different. The journey is long, the climbs can be steep, and the air can feel thin at times. But with vision, steady progress, and a strong team, you'll reach summits that once seemed impossible. And when you do, the view of a thriving culture of well-being is always worth it.

This book began with a bold call: to redefine well-being not as a stand-alone effort or solely an individual's burden but as a strategic necessity embedded into the core of an organization's culture.

In Section One, you explored the shift from reactive care to proactive, systems-level leadership. You also learned about the evolution of health promotion from isolated efforts to integrated strategies, making the case for health-promoting organizations not just as an ideal but as an attainable and essential goal, grounded in both public health principles and personal belief.

Section Two presented the practical blueprint: the five rings of the Harrington Well-Being Model—WHY, WHO, WHAT, HOW, and WHEN. Together, they provide a flexible framework to guide strategic planning and daily decisions. These rings help you define and clarify your purpose, involve stakeholders, select wellness dimensions, integrate strategies across levels, and allocate efforts along a meaningful continuum of care. They support understanding complexity while honoring the humanity at the core of this work.

The final chapters shifted into action, where frameworks became tools and strategy met storytelling. You learned how to build high-performing teams, craft resonant messaging, and measure what matters—not just to track progress but also to tell the story of transformation. You explored how alignment, visibility, and trust can generate momentum and resources. And you gained examples, language, and structure to connect your vision to your organization's reality.

But now it's time to focus on the most important part of your professional success—your health and well-being. You!

This work is personal—and so is the cost.

You're not just designing strategies or launching programs; you're holding space for others. You're carrying stories of struggle and strength. You're supporting people through burnout, change, and uncertainty. You're advocating in rooms that don't always speak your language or see your vision. And often, you're doing this without a full team, a formal title, or a clear road map. This isn't a complaint—it's the reality of leading culture change.

Let's be honest: This path is not for the faint of heart. It demands more from you than most roles—patience, resilience, creativity, and sometimes outright bravery. You're navigating outdated assumptions, shrinking budgets, structural silos, and shifting expectations. You may be the only one in the room with a wellness perspective—sometimes the only one who sees that well-being is the common thread, not an extra. And yet here you are, still showing up and still planting seeds.

> You are helping shape a future where care and connection are integral to how organizations operate, and that selfless work needs you at your best.

This Chapter Is for You

This chapter isn't just about tools; it's about nourishment. It's about remembering that this work, while challenging, is sacred. You're shaping a future where care and connection aren't just nice ideas—they're built into the very fabric of how organizations operate. That kind of change can't be measured only by participation rates or downloads. It needs you at your best.

So let's talk about that—how to maintain your sense of wholeness while encouraging it in others. True leadership means guiding in a sustainable, joyful, and courageous manner. You are your most valuable asset, and you also need to prioritize self-care. Taking care of yourself isn't selfish; it's essential for effective leadership. You can't demonstrate resilience if you're burnt out or promote wellness if you're depleted. Remember the flight-safety rule: Put your oxygen mask on first. Whatever helps you stay centered—a walk outside, meditation, prayer, journaling, gravel-biking, or gardening—protect it as you would any important meeting.

You're not here just to run programs or manage calendars. You're here to transform culture—linking well-being with leadership, belonging, and purpose. That work requires boldness and gentleness, strategy and compassion. And yes, it can feel lonely—like shouting into the wind or saying the same thing for the hundredth time.

This is your pause. Your breath. Your reminder. You've been building the system—now let's create sustainability for you, the human behind the blueprint.

Well-Being Starts with You

If there's one thing wellness leaders struggle with most, it's practicing what we preach. We promote rest, balance, connection, and self-care…yet we also skip meals, push through exhaustion, and check emails at midnight. Sound familiar? But here's the truth: You can't model well-being while running on fumes. You can't build a culture of care if you aren't taking care of yourself. And you definitely can't sustain this work long-term if your tank is empty. Taking care of yourself isn't indulgent; it's leadership. It's strategic. It's how you show up with clarity, presence, and compassion. When you protect your energy, you safeguard your ability to lead.

For me, that includes early morning meditation, gardening, getting dirty on gravel-bike rides, and saying no when I need to. I schedule thinking time on my calendar and protect it like any other appointment. When I feel stuck, I journal. Before tough conversations, I breathe deeply. These aren't luxuries; they're essential skills. They're my anchors in the chaos.

So take a walk in the middle of the day. Eat your lunch without any screens or stacks of paper to look at. Sit in the sun. Cancel the meeting if needed. You are not a robot, and your energy isn't limitless. Give yourself permission to pause. Listen to what your mind, body, and spirit need—and honor it.

Use the Model for Yourself

Throughout this book, you've explored the Harrington Well-Being Model as a strategic guide for organizations. But what if you applied that same lens inward?

Tips from My Journey to Help You Thrive, Personally and Professionally

1. **Start with your WHY.** Why did I choose this path? What purpose drives my passion?

    When you reconnect with your core reason for doing this, it becomes your compass, especially when challenges arise.

2. **Now think about your WHO.** Who are my people—the ones who encourage me, challenge me, remind me of my worth?

    Identify your cheerleaders and stay connected to them. This work cannot be done alone.

3. **Then consider your WHAT.** Which aspects of my well-being need attention? Physical? Emotional? Spiritual? Creative?

    It's okay to admit you've missed something. That awareness is the first step toward realignment.

4. **Reflect on your HOW.** Am I showing up for myself in meaningful ways—across the individual, interpersonal, and organizational levels? Am I surrounded by environments that support or drain me?

5. **And finally, consider your WHEN.** Am I taking charge of my wellness or just reacting when things hit a crisis? Am I waiting for the perfect moment to rest, recharge, or reflect?

    (Spoiler: The perfect moment never arrives. Start now.)

The model isn't just a blueprint; it's a mirror. Use it to see where you are and where you need to go—not just as a leader but as a human being navigating complexity with courage.

Use Constructive Reframing to Shape Your Reality

Let's discuss resistance—whether from others or even yourself. How many times have you heard (or said) "I love this idea, **but** we don't have the time/money/support"? It's one of the most common obstacles in this work. Yet there's a simple change that can make a big difference. Try replacing the big *but* with an *and/so*.

Instead of "**But** we don't have the budget," say, "**And** we don't have the budget, **so** let's get creative with in-kind resources."

Instead of "**But** leadership isn't on board," say, "**And** leadership isn't on board yet, **so** that gives us the chance to build momentum with early adopters."

Instead of "**But** I have so much to do," say, "**And** I have so much to do, **so** I will make a list of what I can get done today."

And as you consider your "so" solutions, filter them through the HOW model: Which strategies are individual, which are organizational, which are policy—and which require a mix?

This isn't just wordplay; it's a mindset shift. It moves you and others from obstacles to action, from frustration to possibility. It helps you and others discover your lane of influence and move forward with what you can do. It's a reminder that barriers can also be bridges if you choose to see them that way.

Every time you encounter a big BUT, pause first. Ask yourself: How might I reframe this? What's the next small step? It's one of the most powerful tools in your leadership tool kit.

And speaking of small steps—remember, culture change is a marathon, not a microwave dinner. It doesn't emerge fully formed in three minutes. It's more like building a savings account or getting fit: You can't sprint your way to long-term results. Instead, it's those steady deposits—one conversation here, one policy tweak there—that add up.

It took years to get where things are today, and the progress you're making now is like interest compounding. Some days will feel like slow motion; other days, you'll be surprised by how much you've progressed. The secret? Keep moving forward. Don't wait for perfection—because your 80% is someone else's 100%.

If something isn't moving as quickly as you hoped—or at all (and it will happen, probably more than you'd like)—don't despair. Fall gracefully, reflect, and learn. Priorities shift inside and outside organizations, and there will be seasons when well-being isn't centered. Your work still matters, and progress is still possible—even if it looks different from what you had planned. Lean on your strengths and support systems; reach out to colleagues and friends. Keep iterating, adapting, and moving forward.

Keep making those small deposits into your culture-change bank, celebrate each little win, and trust that the balance is growing. Before you know it, you'll be standing in the middle of a thriving culture, wondering when it all added up. (Spoiler: It already has—you just didn't see it growing.)

Celebrate the Small Wins

Your job can feel like eating an elephant—impossible. But as the punchline to the old joke "How do you eat an elephant?" goes, "One bite at a time."

Reaching for the low-hanging fruit for small, incremental wins that align with your organizational WHY is the place to start. What's one visible, doable change you can make this month? Maybe it's adding a wellness check-in to team meetings. Perhaps it's aligning your language across departments. Maybe it's bringing together two siloed groups for a shared conversation. These small acts are not just symbolic—they're strategic. They create early wins, build trust, and lay the groundwork for bigger changes.

Culture change is subtle. Sometimes you don't notice it until you look back. That's why it's so important to track and name progress along the way.

The colleague who starts using the language of well-being—that's a win.

The committee that begins its meeting with gratitude or reflection—that's momentum.

The first time someone says, "I think this could be a well-being strategy"—that's a cultural shift in motion.

Don't wait for big milestones to celebrate. Highlight the ripples. Share them in newsletters, meetings, and one-on-one chats to raise awareness and boost engagement. These moments prove your strategy works and inspire those who might still be doubtful.

Remember, you're doing more than just starting initiatives. You're reshaping mindsets and weaving a culture of care into your organization's fabric, often without a clear road map or a title that matches your impact. And let's be honest, often while trying to do it all.

You're not alone in that experience. Change in work culture can feel isolating—like shouting into the wind or planting seeds with no guarantee they'll grow. But that's not failure; that's the root system taking hold.

Think about bamboo. It spends years growing underground before anything appears above the surface. Then, seemingly overnight, it shoots up strong and fast. That's the work you're doing: quiet, powerful, unseen by many. You might not be getting applause now, but you are laying the foundation. One day, the growth will be undeniable. Pole, pole.

Your Sound Bites Matter

In boardrooms, hallways, and elevator rides, you may only have seconds to make your case. That's why clear, memorable sound bites are essential—short, impactful lines that explain what you do and why it matters. You are the steward of this work, the subject matter expert who carries both the vision and credibility to back it up. One of my favorite sound bites: "NIOSH advises against lifting more than 50 pounds, but nurses do it dozens of times a day." That single line sparked more awareness than any lengthy report ever could.

Your words don't need to be flashy; they just need to land. Combine data with a human story. Pair a statistic with a real-life example. Lead with clarity, speak sincerely.

Ask yourself what is your WHY and answer in one sentence. What's the impact? Why should it matter to both individuals and the organization? When you can answer those questions clearly, you position yourself not just as a contributor but also as the trusted voice shaping the conversation.

A few final thoughts on communication: Always assume positive intent, be kind, be curious, be professional…and communicate, communicate, communicate. What you have to say matters.

Embrace the Spiral

At some point, you'll reach the messy middle. Things that once felt exciting may now seem stuck. Priorities will change. People will move on. You'll face the same challenge more than once. This doesn't mean you're failing; it means you're growing. My mom calls this messy middle the "teenage years"—that awkward time we have to get through.

Progress isn't a straight line; it's a spiral. Each time you revisit a familiar point, you do so with more insight, clarity, and new tools. What seems like starting over is actually an opportunity to grow. That spiral symbolizes your evolution. Trust it. Be gentle with yourself amid the chaos. You are not falling behind; you are transforming. Yes, you'll revisit this work again and again. That's the nature of transformation. But each time you return, you're gaining more wisdom, new perspectives, and a stronger foundation. And remember, much of this work unfolds in its own time.

When things feel slow, remember listening, assessing, building trust—that *is* the work. This isn't "extra" or "nice to have." It's what you were brought in to do.

Take the time to "weed the garden." Do the assessments. Walk the halls, sit in on meetings, and do your meet and greets. Learn the acronyms, the personalities, the pockets of resistance and energy. These are not distractions from your goal; they are your strategy. Stay curious, stay grounded, stay humble. This is a long game that spirals around and around, and you are right where you need to be. Each spiral is a little higher, a little further along.

And don't forget what brought you joy. When you feel stuck, come back to your WHY. Reconnect with the reason you started this work. Joy is not a distraction from the mission; it's the fuel that sustains it.

Build Your Village, Find Your People

When I became a CWO, I didn't know many others in similar roles. At that time, there was no guidebook or pre-made network. So in addition to relying on local friends and colleagues, I started building the professional community I needed. For me, it began with a single email to a colleague with a similar role. We exchanged notes, shared resources, and motivated each other to keep going. These conversations can grow into a small, informal circle, adding colleagues along the way—whether from higher education, healthcare, or public health. Soon, the calls become a lifeline—swapping strategy documents and language that resonates with senior leaders, and even creating space to vent.

You can build this too. This work can feel isolating, especially if you're the only "wellness person" in your department or organization, but you don't have to do it alone. Start with the allies already around you. They may be in HR, benefits, sustainability, spiritual life, safety, academic affairs, or student affairs. They may be your local public health departments. They may not have *wellness* or *well-being* in their titles, but they're already fostering care, inclusion, and connection in their work. Invite them to lunch. Form a cross-functional team. Join a professional network. Send the brave email. Ask for a virtual coffee with someone whose work you admire. Those small actions build trust, and over time, they create a web of support that sustains you, sparks new ideas, and keeps the work moving forward.

That's what happened for me—and it was a game changer. This work requires a community, and so do you.

And here's the reminder we all need: You don't have to be the hero. You *are* a hero, but you don't have to do everything. You don't have to know everything. Your job isn't to have every answer—it's to be a catalyst, a conductor, a connector of great work. Borrow language. Adapt templates. Build on what others have done. That's not weakness; it's smart, strategic collaboration.

Stay Curious, Grounded, and Inspired

This field is always changing, and so are you. Keep connected to the spark that brought you here.

In the Air Force, we called it getting "re-blued"—taking time to reconnect with the mission, the purpose, and the heart of the work. You need space for that too. Here are some of the things that remind me.

- Reading works by authors like Vivek Murthy, Atul Gawande, Wendy Lynch, Vic Strecher, Jessica Grossmeier, and Richard Rohr

- Attending my favorite conferences, including the HERO Forum, the National Association of Student Personnel Administrators (NASPA) Strategies, and the Art & Science of Health Promotion

- Starting my mornings with centering prayer or spending a few quiet moments in the garden

- Riding or walking with friends

- Discovering new voices and perspectives, especially those that challenge or surprise me

Make time for whatever re-blues you. Schedule it like a meeting. Treat it like fuel, because it is. Your fire lights the way for others. Keep it tended.

Open up to Gratitude

This final message is from me to you: From the bottom of my heart, thank you—for showing up, staying curious, challenging the status quo, and choosing to do the difficult yet human and meaningful work of culture change. Thank you for continuing the journey and shaping the future of health-promoting organizations. I am deeply grateful to you.

You are the connector. The conductor. The change agent. The culture-shifter. I hope this book helps you continue to make it happen and encourages you to connect with other Mollie/Mike Make-It-Happen types within your organization and beyond. Thank you for making it yours, making it happen, and above all—making it matter.

Make It Yours! Make It Happen!

You've studied the model, the mindset, the methods—and now it's time to bring them into your world. On your terms. In your voice. With your community. So here's your invitation to exercise all you've learned in this book.

1. Begin with what's achievable. Pilot a small project. Share a new framework. Invite someone to join the conversation.

2. Adapt what you've learned. This book was never intended as a prescription; it's a springboard. Take what resonates with you. Adjust what fits your situation. Let go of what doesn't.

3. Keep building connections. Use this framework to align, elevate, and inspire throughout your organization.

4. Remain true to your WHY. Let your values and vision steer you through the chaos, uncertainty, and wonder.

This work is messy. It's powerful. It's personal. And it's yours to shape. You don't need to wait for the perfect moment. Just pick one place to start. Pole, pole…one bite at a time.

ABOUT THE AUTHOR

Dr. Suzy Harrington began her career as an Air Force nurse and has spent decades advancing health and well-being across clinical, educational, and organizational systems. With a master's degree in health promotion, earned before "wellness" was even a mainstream concept, and a Doctor of Nursing Practice focused on healthcare leadership and business strategy, her work has evolved from individual care to prevention education, and ultimately to system-wide transformation.

Dr. Harrington's career has been shaped by both her military service and her experiences as a military spouse, leading to a breadth of leadership roles in diverse and dynamic settings. She served as the Air Force's Health Promotion Subject Matter Expert and later as Director of the Department of Health, Safety, and Wellness at the American Nurses Association.

She was recruited to become the first dedicated CWO in higher education at Oklahoma State University, where she helped shape and embed foundational well-being strategies. This pioneering work led to leadership roles in launching and advancing health-promoting campus movements at Oklahoma State, Georgia Tech, and the University of Houston.

Dr. Harrington has held executive roles in both higher education and healthcare, including serving as Assistant Vice President over integrated student well-being services—ranging from student health and counseling to campus recreation and disability services—and leading workforce well-being efforts within a major healthcare system. There she oversaw strategic and operational expansion of programs supporting benefits, medical services, employee assistance, chaplaincy, and engagement initiatives.

A nationally recognized thought leader, Dr. Harrington contributed to the creation of the Okanagan Charter: An International Charter for Health-Promoting Universities & Colleges and has served on multiple national and international boards advancing whole-system well-being. Her work continues to influence wellness leaders across sectors.

Most recently, she held two high-impact interim consulting roles: first as Interim Executive Director of Student Well-Being at the University of Vermont, and then at the University of Houston, where she was invited back to elevate and realign their health-promotion strategies.

Now retired from full-time leadership roles, Dr. Harrington devotes her time to consulting, teaching, and writing—supporting the next generation of well-being leaders and helping organizations embed health and well-being into their core strategy, operations, and culture.

ACKNOWLEDGMENTS

This book wouldn't exist without the amazing community of health and well-being professionals and collaborators I've been lucky to work with over the years. To every well-being professional out there—those who bring heart, hustle, and hope to building health-promoting organizations—your creativity, grit, and unwavering commitment to this complex work inspire me every day.

Special thanks to my colleagues in Air Force Health Promotion, whose dedication instilled discipline and vision; to the American Nurses Association, where I saw the power of collective advocacy; and to the many hospitals and universities that shaped my understanding of organizational health. To Oklahoma State University, where the idea of a CWO first took root, thank you for your early trust and courage. To the University of Houston, where I returned to see innovation flourish. Your energy and resilience are woven throughout these pages.

To the students, employees, and community members who showed up, spoke up, and gave honest feedback—your voices are the heartbeat of this work, reminding me that well-being is lived, not just theorized.

To the visionary leaders and passionate teams in HERO and the U.S. Health-Promoting Campuses Network, thank you for creating environments where wellness can thrive on a large scale, and for advancing the field with bold ideas and practical solutions.

To the countless wellness committees and coworkers who collaborated, debated, and refined these ideas with me, you showed me the strength of teamwork and the skill of compromise in creating lasting change.

To my pre-readers, especially Michael Grimsley, Dr. Bridget Weikel, and Dr. Janis Davis-Street, whose thoughtful critiques improved the quality and clarity of this book: Your generosity and insights made all the difference.

To my friends, who graciously accepted that sometimes my priorities meant skipping bike rides or social outings, your patience and understanding provided me with the time I needed to write.

To Dr. Jess Grossmeier—my walking buddy, book partner, and purpose-filled friend—our conversations wove meaning, connection, spirituality, and direction into this work. Your generous and unwavering support has been a constant source of strength and inspiration.

To Chris Dawe, who helped bring form and clarity to my ideas, your encouragement and thoughtful feedback sharpened the work and supported me throughout this journey. I'm deeply grateful for your steady presence and insight.

To Lynn Sparrow Christy, who has been more than a spiritual advisor, a true friend and mentor, thank you for your unwavering presence and supportive friendship.

To Dr. Sue Swider, who served as my mentor during my doctoral studies and is a passionate advocate for public health. Her visionary leadership and involvement with the National Prevention Strategy helped shape the vision of the Harrington Well-Being Model.

Acknowledgments

And finally, to my mom, my anchor and best friend, whose love, strength, and endless support have been the foundation of everything I am and do. Thank you for walking beside me through every high and low, every doubt and triumph.

This book is for all of us who embrace our individuality while coming together as we are *making it happen*—turning vision into reality, one courageous step at a time.

Heartfelt thanks to the many colleagues, leaders, and friends who were early readers and shared thoughtful words of support for my book. Additional praise and reflections can be found at **SuzyHarrington.com**.

ADDITIONAL RESOURCES GUIDE

This guide is not comprehensive and is not meant to cover every model, framework, or thought leader in the field. Instead, it highlights some of the resources that have significantly influenced my own work and that I wish I had known about when I began my well-being journey.

Think of it as a living tool kit—a collection you can explore whenever you need fresh ideas, language, or perspectives. You might use it when you are creating a new initiative, seeking ways to approach a conversation with leadership, or simply looking for inspiration when the work feels challenging.

I've organized these resources into five sections:

- **Core Health-Promotion Concepts:** Start here to learn more about the field of health promotion and where these concepts fit into the levels of the rings.

- **Key Terms to Shape Perspective:** Use this to learn more about some of the terms you might hear and where they fit into the levels of the rings.

- **Organizational Frameworks for Benchmarking Resources:** Use these when aligning with benchmarks, policies, or accreditation requirements.

- **Planning and Tracking Tools:** Use these when planning, mapping, or tracking progress.

- **People and Places for Inspiration:** Use these when you need fresh ideas, role models, or opportunities to connect with peers.

As the landscape of well-being continues to change, the most relevant tools will also evolve. I hope this resource will inspire creativity and connect you with approaches that align with your unique WHO, WHAT, WHY, WHEN, and HOW.

Core Health-Promotion Concepts

Foundational models that explain behavior and well-being, helping leaders develop more innovative strategies; start here to learn more about the field of health promotion.

Individual-Focused

» **Health Belief Model** WHO, HOW, WHEN
A cornerstone framework that helps predict and explain *individual* health behaviors through six components: Perceived Susceptibility, Perceived Severity, Perceived Benefits, Perceived Barriers, Cues to Action, and Self-Efficacy. It is highly adaptable for designing prevention and promotion programs.

Where It Helps: Crafting targeted communications, reducing barriers, and designing prompts (nudges)

» **Hierarchy of Needs (Maslow)** WHO, WHAT, WHEN
A motivational framework that categorizes human needs into five levels: physiological, safety, love & belonging, esteem, and self-actualization; provides insight for designing strategies that support not only survival but also growth and fulfillment.

Where It Helps: Identifying and ensuring critical low-level needs are met

» **Stages of Change (Transtheoretical Model)** WHO, HOW, WHEN
A six-stage process that includes Precontemplation, Contemplation, Preparation, Action, Maintenance, and Termination; recognizing individuals' readiness to change helps tailor interventions to their actual states rather than assumptions.

Pro Tip: Match messages to readiness (for example, awareness stories for contemplation or how-to checklists for preparation).

Community-Focused

» **Diffusion of Innovation (Rogers)** WHO, HOW, WHEN
Explains how new ideas and practices spread within communities and organizations; identifies adopter categories: Innovators (2.5%), Early Adopters (13.5%), Early Majority (34%), Late Majority (34%), and Laggards (16%); provides practical guidance for scaling initiatives by customizing strategies for different audiences.

Pro Tip: Spot early adopters to champion the work.

» **Socio-Ecological Model (SEM) HOW**
Demonstrates that behavior is influenced across multiple levels: individual, interpersonal, organizational, community/environment, and policy; emphasizes that sustainable change requires interventions at various levels.

Where It Helps: Designing multi-level strategies that outlast leadership changes

Dimension-Focused

» **Gallup's Five Elements of Well-Being WHAT**
Elements include career, social, financial, physical, community; research shows that career well-being (purposeful work) is the strongest predictor of overall life satisfaction.

Pro Tip: Start with Career/Purpose to generate momentum in other areas.

» **Mental Health Continuum (Keyes) WHO, WHEN**
Highlights mental health as more than just the absence of illness, ranging from languishing to moderate to flourishing.

Where It Helps: Setting goals beyond "reduced distress" toward "more flourishing"

» **PERMA Model (Seligman) HOW, WHEN**
Five elements—Positive Emotion, Engagement, Relationships, Meaning, and Accomplishment—form the

foundation of flourishing; a practical tool for program assessment and individual growth.

Quick Example: Map programs to PERMA (such as Recognition → Accomplishment).

Key Terms to Shape Perspective

Big ideas that reshape how we view health, equity, and culture; use this to learn more about some of the terms you might hear.

» **Health in All Policies (HiAP)** WHO, HOW, WHEN
A cross-sector approach that ensures health considerations are incorporated into policy decisions across all sectors, such as transportation, housing, and education; recognizes that factors outside healthcare impact overall well-being.

Where It Helps: Cross-department planning and demonstrating that everyone has a role

» **Salutogenesis (Antonovsky)** WHEN
A paradigm shift that emphasizes factors promoting health rather than merely preventing illness; its core concept, sense of coherence, highlights life as understandable, manageable, and meaningful.

Where It Helps: Reframing programming from focusing on deficits to emphasizing assets and designing resilience-oriented approaches

» **Universal Design** WHO, WHY, HOW
Ensures that environments, communications, and systems are accessible to everyone, regardless of age, ability, or background; shifts the focus from merely accommodating to honestly expecting inclusion.

Quick Example: Shoveling the ramp

» **Upstream, Midstream, Downstream** WHEN
A metaphor and public health principles emphasizing proactive strategies that address the root causes of health and well-being, rather than reacting to crises downstream; going upstream means creating conditions that prevent harm, build resilience, and foster environments where people can thrive—such as addressing social determinants of health, implementing policy changes, or modifying cultural norms—before problems occur; often contrasted with midstream (prevention and risk reduction) and downstream (treatment and crisis response).

Quick Example: Update scheduling policies (upstream) versus offering stress classes (midstream) versus employee assistance program counseling (downstream).

» **WIIFM (What's In It For Me)** WHO
A communications principle that reminds leaders to emphasize relevance and personal benefits when engaging others; plays a crucial role in transforming abstract strategies into personal significance.

Pro Tip: Look for a win-win.

» **World Health Organization (W.H.O.) Health Promotion Glossary of Terms, 2021** HOW, WHEN
Provides an updated, significantly revised set of concise definitions for key health-promotion concepts to standardize language across policy, practice, and research; includes new and modified terms with explanatory notes and links to sources.

Pro Tip: Use this as your terminology "style guide" when unsure of a definition.

Organizational Frameworks and Benchmarking Resources

Global charters, policy frameworks, and industry standards that set practice benchmarks; use these when aligning with benchmarks, policies, or accreditation requirements.

Global Charters & Frameworks

» **Geneva Charter for Well-Being (W.H.O. 2021)**
Calls for societies to prioritize well-being through five global actions: valuing the planet, creating fair economies, integrating healthy public policies, ensuring universal health coverage, and managing digital changes wisely.

Pro Tip: Use this as a framing slide for executive briefings on "why well-being now."

- » **Limerick Framework for Action (2025)**
  A renewal of the Okanagan Charter that offers a global tool kit to embed well-being into institutional culture, operations, and academic vitality; connects health promotion with sustainability, equity, and education.

  Where It Helps: Future-proofing campus strategy for health in all policies

- » **Okanagan Charter: Health-Promoting Campuses (2015)**
  Two calls to action: embed health into all aspects of campus culture and lead health promotion locally and globally; offers a unifying vision for higher education worldwide.

  Quick Example: Connect curriculum, operations, and student life to a shared health goal.

- » **Ottawa Charter for Health Promotion (1986)**
  Foundational W.H.O. charter establishing five key action areas: building healthy public policy, creating supportive environments, strengthening community action, developing personal skills, and reorienting health services.

  Where It Helps: Orientation to the field; building a shared North Star

Workplace & Healthcare Tools

- » **American Medical Association (AMA) Joy in Medicine Recognition Program**
  Promotes system-level efforts to decrease burnout in health care.

Quick Example: Align chief warrant officer priorities with Joy in Medicine domains.

» **C. Everett Koop National Health Awards**
Recognizes organizations that demonstrate evidence-based outcomes and business impact.

Where It Helps: Set ambition; study awardees for replicable practices

» **Health Enhancement Research Organization (HERO) Scorecard**
Free benchmarking tool that evaluates leadership, culture, incentives, communication, and outcomes.

Pro Tip: Use it annually to show year-over-year changes on three to five key items.

» **International Organization for Standardization (ISO) 45003**
The first global standard for managing psychosocial risks; provides guidance for creating psychologically safe workplaces.

Quick Example: Incorporate risk assessments for workload, role clarity, and civility.

» **National Institute for Occupational Safety and Health (NIOSH) Total Worker Health**
Combines safety and well-being; tackles physical and psychosocial risks together.

Pro Tip: Pair safety committees with well-being councils for collaborative efforts.

Higher Education & Campus Well-Being

» **Active Minds' Healthy Campus Award**
Recognizes excellence in student mental health promotion.

Pro Tip: Use award criteria as a gap analysis checklist.

» **American College Health Association (ACHA) Healthy Campus Framework**
Aligns campus strategies with Healthy People 2030 and includes benchmarking tools.

Where It Helps: Setting campus-wide goals and shared indicators

» **Council for the Advancement of Standards (CAS)**
Functional standards, including health promotion, to support self-assessment and improvement.

Quick Example: Map unit outcomes to CAS learning domains.

» **JED Campus Framework**
A comprehensive approach to resilience, system alignment, and suicide prevention.

Where It Helps: Cross-silo mental health strategy and postvention planning

US Public Health Tools

» **Center for Disease Control and Prevention (CDC) PLACES**
Optional to add alongside CHRR if used often; small-area estimates for local planning; highlights hidden inequities.

Pro Tip: Layer PLACES maps with internal HR or student data for better targeting.

» **Center for Disease Control and Prevention (CDC) Worksite Health ScoreCard**
Includes 154 yes/no items across 16 topics; compares progress to national standards.

Pro Tip: Use annually; show year-over-year movement on three to five priority items.

» **County Health Rankings & Roadmaps (CHRR)**
Ranks county health; offers tools and partner guidance.

Quick Example: Use local data to prioritize upstream actions with community partners.

» **Healthy People 2030 (HP2030)**
National, measurable objectives (determinants, prevention, equity, resilience).

Pro Tip: Identify three to five HP2030 measures to anchor your dashboard.

- » **The National Prevention Strategy (2011)**
  Shift from treatment to prevention, outlining four strategic directions and seven priorities.

  Where It Helps: Provides strategic narratives for boards and councils.

Planning and Tracking Tools

Practical tools that assist leaders in designing, assessing, and enhancing well-being initiatives; use these when planning, mapping, or tracking progress.

- » **Collaboration Spectrum (Liz Weaver)**
  Identifies stages of collaboration from siloed to integrated.

  Pro Tip: Use the graph to show how cross-cultural siloed efforts can align.

- » **Collective Impact Framework**
  Identifies five conditions to optimize impact: Common Agenda, Shared Measurement, Mutually Reinforcing Activities, Continuous Communication, and Backbone Organization.

  Quick Example: Use it for system-wide collaboration.

- » **Crosswalk Tools**
  Map overlaps across models, accreditations, and assessments to reduce redundancy.

Pro Tip: Create a one-page crosswalk to show leaders' alignment and gaps.

» **Journey Mapping**
Visualize participant experience; identify pain points and key moments.

Quick Example: Map "new employee" or "student care navigation" journeys.

» **The Kellogg Logic Model**
Connect inputs, activities, outputs, and outcomes strategically; clarify cause and effect.

Where It Helps: Grant proposals, dashboards, and planning initiatives

» **SWOT Analysis**
Identify strengths, weaknesses, opportunities, and threats both internally and externally; great place to start.

Pro Tip: Highlight strengths and opportunities in planning.

Individual Based Survey & Assessment Tools

» **Flourishing Scale (Diener):** Brief snapshot of relationships, purpose, optimism, and self-esteem.

» **Gallup Well-Being Index:** Benchmark across five validated areas.

» **PERMA-Profiler (Butler & Kern):** A 15-item measure assessing PERMA factors: Positive Emotion, Engagement, Relationships, Meaning, and Accomplishment.

Where They Help: Pre- and post-evaluations, subgroup insights, and storytelling with data

Quality & Systems Improvement

» **Institute of Medicine's (IOM) Six Aims:** Safe, Effective, Patient-Centered, Timely, Efficient, Equitable

» **PDCA (Plan/Do/Check/Act):** Small tests of change; repeatable learning cycles.

Quick Example: Pilot one clinic/department; scale after "Check/Act"

» **Triple Aim / Quadruple Aim:** Patient experience, population health, cost; plus workforce well-being

Where They Help: Balance metrics to prevent sacrificing staff well-being for throughput.

People and Places for Inspiration

Thought leaders, reflective voices, and professional gatherings that shape the field; use these when you need fresh ideas, role models, or opportunities to connect with peers.

Thought Leaders & Key Influencers

» **Mark Dooris**
A leading scholar in health-promoting universities; developed comprehensive systems approaches that integrate health into institutional structures, campus operations, and academic

culture; co-created the UK Healthy Universities Self-Review Tool, which remains a model for institutional assessment; work demonstrates that higher education institutions are not only places of learning but also settings that directly influence and exemplify community well-being.

Try This: Use his self-review approach to start your campus-wide conversation.

» **Atul Gawande**
Surgeon, author, and public health leader whose writing clarifies complex issues in the health system; work emphasizes improving healthcare delivery, patient safety, and the compassionate side of medicine; studies on aging, end-of-life care, and system improvements have changed how leaders and clinicians think about quality of care.

Pro Tip: Assign an article or chapter for leadership rounds to encourage better quality improvement discussions.

» **Ron Goetzel**
A pioneer in measuring workplace health promotion; his Value on Investment (VOI) framework goes beyond financial ROI by emphasizing the importance of culture, employee engagement, and organizational mission; work helped legitimize well-being programs in the eyes of businesses and policymakers.

Try This: Pair VOI with a few "hard" key performance indicators to satisfy finance and HR.

- **Jessica Grossmeier**
  Researcher and thought leader who blends evidence-based well-being practices with management science and workplace spirituality; work emphasizes purpose-driven well-being by integrating metrics, culture, and higher meaning; creates practical tools for assessing, aligning, and sustaining organizational well-being.

  Pro Tip: Use her purpose/connection/transcendence perspective in leader workshops.

- **Wendy Lynch**
  Expert in translating complex data into insights that influence decision-making and human performance; bridges the gap between analytics and storytelling, helping leaders demonstrate the business case for well-being while staying grounded in human experience.

  Try This: Turn one spreadsheet into a one-slide "insight + action" story.

- **Renee Moorefield**
  Cofounder and CEO of Wisdom Works Group and the creator of the Be Well Lead Well platform; advocates for leaders to prioritize their own well-being in order to maintain thriving organizations; frameworks focus on resilient leadership, human sustainability, and global vitality.

  Pro Tip: Pilot a leader cohort using Be Well Lead Well measures.

» **Vivek Murthy**
U.S. Surgeon General during the nineteenth and twenty-first terms; emphasized social connection and happiness as key public health priorities; advice on loneliness redefined isolation not as a private issue but as a societal epidemic with serious health risks; work links mental, social, and physical health, demonstrating that policy must address all aspects.

Try This: Add connection indicators to your well-being dashboard.

» **Richard Rohr**
Franciscan priest and globally respected teacher who emphasizes spirituality, wholeness, and inner transformation as essential for resilience and purpose; insights offer leaders a foundation in meaning-making that enhances systems-level strategies.

Pro Tip: Use a brief reflection or question from Rohr to start retreats.

» **Martin Seligman**
The father of positive psychology; developed the PERMA model and emphasized the difference between flourishing and languishing; work is fundamental for both individual well-being and organizational culture strategies.

Try This: Build a PERMA audit of current programs.

» **Simon Sinek**
Leadership theorist who popularized the Golden Circle framework: Why–How–What; work demonstrates the power

of starting with purpose to foster ownership, belonging, and transformation; insights help leaders create resonance rather than mere compliance.

Quick Example: Start every change plan with a crisp WHY statement.

» **Vic Strecher**
Researcher focused on purpose and its connection to health, longevity, and resilience; his research indicates that having a purpose can extend lifespan and improve quality of life by lowering disease risk and promoting better sleep.

Pro Tip: Incorporate personal purpose exercises into onboarding or leadership programs.

» **Paul Wesselmann ("The Ripples Guy")**
Speaker and educator who makes resilience tangible and relatable; his Four-Stage Resilience Model—Reaching IN, Reaching OUT, Surviving & Reviving, Thriving Forward—helps individuals and organizations frame growth through challenges; metaphor-rich "ripples" approach emphasizes small acts building toward broader cultural waves.

Try This: Open meetings with a "small ripple" prompt to build habits.

Professional Development & Conferences

» **American College Health Association (ACHA) Annual Meeting**
Largest gathering of college health professionals; features evidence-based education, professional development, and benchmarking; focuses on student health services, prevention, and well-being.

» **American Public Health Association (APHA) Annual Meeting & Expo**
Top US public health event; brings together researchers, practitioners, and policymakers for science, advocacy, and cross-sector collaboration.

» **Art and Science of Health-Promotion Conference**
Multidisciplinary, combining rigorous peer review with practical applications across sectors from fitness to executive leadership.

» **Health Enhancement Research Organization (HERO) Forum**
Flagship employer health event linking business leaders with scientists and practitioners; focused on measurement and practical playbooks.

» **National Association of Student Personnel Administrators (NASPA) Strategies Conferences**
Convergence of five specialized events (Mental Health, Violence Prevention, Alcohol/Drugs, Peer Education, Well-

Being/Health-Promotion Leadership); premier student affairs event for health and wellness leaders in higher education.

» **National Wellness Institute Annual Conference**
Multisector wellness community; whole-person focus with continuing education opportunities.

» **Wellness Council of America (WELCOA) Summit**
Employer wellness leaders share practical strategies and case studies for creating cultures of health.

ENDNOTES

1. Sinek, Simon. 2011. *Start with Why: How Great Leaders Inspire Everyone to Take Action*. Penguin Books.

2. Starbucks Coffee Company. 2025. "Our Starbucks Mission." January 9, 2025. https://about.starbucks.com/stories/2025/our-starbucks-mission/.

3. Maslow, Abraham H. 1943. "A Theory of Human Motivation." *Psychological Review* 50 (4): 370–96. https://doi.org/10.1037/h0054346.

4. Christesen, Paul. 2009. "Whence 776? The Origin of the Date for the First Olympiad." *The International Journal of the History of Sport* 26 (2): 161–82. https://doi.org/10.1080/09523360802511029.

5. Hankinson, R. J. 1998. "Hippocratic Medicine." In *Routledge Encyclopedia of Philosophy*. DOI:10.4324/9780415249126-A060-1.

6. Yannopoulos, Stavros, and Asimina Kaiafa-Saropoulou. 2019. "Hygiene Technologies, Water, and Health in the Hellenic World." In *Healthcare Access – Regional Overviews*, edited by Umar Bacha, Urška Rozman, and Sonja Šostar Turk. IntechOpen. https://doi.org/10.5772/intechopen.90144.

7. Rosen, George. 2015. *A History of Public Health*. Expanded edition. Johns Hopkins University Press.

8. Acquire Publications. 2023. "Lifestyle Changes and Chronic Disease During Industrialization." *Journal of Case Reports and Medical History*. https://www.acquirepublications.org/Journal/CaseReports/PDF/JCRMH2300131.pdf.

9. Mokdad AH, et al. 2004. "Actual Causes of Death in the United States, 2000." Journal of American Medical Association 291 (10): 1238–45. doi:10.1001/jama.291.10.1238.

10. Nielsen SJ, and Barry Popkin. 2003. "Patterns and Trends in Food Portion Sizes, 1977–1998." Journal of American Medical Association 289 (4): 450–3. doi:10.1001/jama.289.4.450.

11 Yao T, et al. 2018. "Healthcare Costs Attributable to Secondhand Smoke Exposure at Home for U.S. Adults." *Preventive Medicine* 108: 41–6. https://doi.org/10.1016/j.ypmed.2017.12.028..

12 World Health Organization. 1946. *Preamble to the Constitution of WHO as Adopted by the International Health Conference*, New York, 19–22 June 1946.

13 Antonovsky, Aaron. 1996. "The Salutogenic Model as a Theory to Guide Health Promotion." *Health Promotion International* 11 (1): 11–18. https://doi.org/10.1093/heapro/11.1.11.

14 Goetzel, Ron Z., et al. 2014. "Do Workplace Health Promotion (Wellness) Programs Work?" *Journal of Occupational and Environmental Medicine* 56 (9): 927–34. https://doi.org/10.1097/JOM.0000000000000276.

15 Maslow, Abraham H. 1943. "A Theory of Human Motivation." *Psychological Review* 50 (4): 370–96. https://doi.org/10.1037/h0054346.

16 Maguire, Angus. 2013. *Equity vs. Equality vs. Justice Illustration*. Interaction Institute for Social Change. https://interactioninstitute.org/illustrating-equality-vs-equity/.

17 U.S. Department of Health and Human Services. 2023. "Our Epidemic of Loneliness and Isolation: The U.S. Surgeon General's Advisory on the Healing Effects of Social Connection and Community." May 2023. https://pubmed.ncbi.nlm.nih.gov/37792968/.

18 World Health Organization. 2021. *Health Promotion Glossary of Terms 2021*. https://www.who.int/publications/i/item/9789240038349.

19 Rath, Tom, and Jim Harter. 2010. *Wellbeing: The Five Essential Elements*. Gallup Press.

20 Keyes, Corey L. M. 2002. "The Mental Health Continuum: From Languishing to Flourishing in Life." *Journal of Health and Social Behavior* 43 (2): 207–22. https://doi.org/10.2307/3090197.

21 Tutu, Desmond. 1999. *No Future Without Forgiveness*. Doubleday.

22 Gallup. 2021. *Social Wellbeing: You Have Meaningful Friendships in Your Life*. https://www.gallup.com/workplace/237020/five-essential-elements.aspx.

23 American Society of Safety Professionals. 2021. *A Guide to ISO 45003: An Overview of the Standard and More Total Worker Health Resources*. https://www.assp.org/docs/default-source/default-document-library/iso_45003_tech_report_final_210703.pdf.

24 Gallup. 2023. *How to Solve Your Student Retention Problem Using Strengths.* https://www.gallup.com/education/544418/solve-student-retention-problem-using-strengths.aspx.

25 Murthy, Vivek. 2015. "US Surgeon General Dr. Vivek Murthy on Gun Violence, Happiness, and More." Speech, June 28, 2015. Spotlight Health, Aspen Ideas Festival. https://www.aspeninstitute.org/blog-posts/us-surgeon-general-vivek-murthy-gun-violence-happiness-more/.

26 Grossmeier, Jessica. 2022. *Reimagining Workplace Well-Being: Fostering a Culture of Purpose, Connection, and Transcendence.* Modern Wisdom Press.

27 Rath, Tom, and Jim Harter. 2010. *Wellbeing: The Five Essential Elements.* Gallup Press.

28 Moorefield, Renee. n.d. *Be Well Lead Well.* Wisdom Works. https://www.wisdom-works.com/.

29 American Nurses Foundation. 2022. *Pulse on the Nation's Nurses COVID-19 Survey Series: Workplace Survey, June–July 2022.* https://www.nursingworld.org/practice-policy/work-environment/health-safety/disaster-preparedness/coronavirus/what-you-need-to-know/covid-19-survey-series-anf-2022-workplace-survey.

30 American Nurses Association. 2013. *Safe Patient Handling and Mobility: Interprofessional National Standards Across the Care Continuum.*

31 Murthy, Vivek H. 2022. *Addressing Health Worker Burnout: The U.S. Surgeon General's Advisory on Building a Thriving Health Workforce.* U.S. Department of Health and Human Services. https://www.hhs.gov/surgeongeneral/reports-and-publications/health-worker-burnout/index.html.

32 Eiseley, Loren. 1968. "The Star Thrower." In *The Unexpected Universe.* Houghton Mifflin Harcourt Publishing Company.

33 Teng, Minnie. 2016. "Frogs in a Pond." *How Teaching Practices Influence Student Mental Health and Wellbeing,* September 7, 2016. https://blogs.ubc.ca/teachingandwellbeing/2016/09/07/frogs-in-a-pond/.

34 World Health Organization. 1986. *Ottawa Charter for Health Promotion.* https://www.who.int/publications/i/item/ottawa-charter-for-health-promotion.

35 World Health Organization. 2016. *Healthy Cities: The Mandate for Healthy Cities.* https://www.who.int/teams/health-promotion/enhanced-wellbeing/ninth-global-conference/healthy-cities.

36 World Health Organization. 2022. *Geneva Charter for Well-being*. https://cdn.who.int/media/docs/default-source/health-promotion/geneva-charter-4-march-2022.pdf.

37 Okanagan Charter: An International Charter for Health Promoting Universities & Colleges. (2015). Developed at the 2015 International Conference on Health Promoting Universities & Colleges, Kelowna, British Columbia. Retrieved from University of British Columbia Library, DOI: 10.14288/1.0132754.

38 University of Limerick. 2023. "Limerick 'Framework for Action' Unveiled at Health Promoting Campus Conference in UL." University of Limerick News. https://www.ul.ie/news/limerick-framework-for-action-unveiled-at-health-promoting-campus-conference-in-ul.

39 American Medical Association. 2020. "Surgery Success Story: Easy Fixes for 'Pebble in Shoe' Problems Have Big Impact." *Steps Forward*, October 15, 2020. https://edhub.ama-assn.org/steps-forward/module/2771513.

40 University of Wisconsin Population Health Institute. 2014. *Explore Health Topics*. County Health Rankings & Roadmaps. https://www.countyhealthrankings.org/explore-health-rankings/measures-data-sources/county-health-rankings-model.

41 Solomon, Mark G., Richard P. Compton, and David F. Preusser. 2004. "Taking the *Click It or Ticket* Model Nationwide." *Journal of Safety Research* 35 (2): 197–201. https://doi.org/10.1016/j.jsr.2004.03.003.

42 World Health Organization. (n.d.). "Promoting Health in All Policies and Intersectoral Action Capacities." World Health Organization. https://www.who.int/activities/promoting-health-in-all-policies-and-intersectoral-action-capacities.

43 Strecher, Victor J. 2016. *Life on Purpose: How Living for What Matters Most Changes Everything*. HarperOne.

44 Gallup. 2017. "Ball State Alumni: Great Jobs and Great Lives – 2017 Undergraduate Alumni Scorecard." Indiana Commission for Higher Education. https://www.in.gov/che/files/Gallup_Indiana_Ball-State-Scorecard_FINAL.PDF.

45 Rogers, Everett M. 2003. *Diffusion of Innovations*. 5th ed. Free Press.

46 U.S. Department of Health and Human Services. 2022. *The U.S. Surgeon General's Framework for Workplace Mental Health & Well-Being*. Office of the Surgeon General. https://www.hhs.gov/sites/default/files/workplace-mental-health-well-being.pdf.

Endnotes

47. Wesselmann, P. (n.d.) WE GOT THIS: Four pillars of resilience [Framework]. The Ripples Guy. https://theripplesguy.com/.

48. Okanagan Charter: An International Charter for Health Promoting Universities & Colleges. (2015). Developed at the 2015 International Conference on Health Promoting Universities & Colleges, Kelowna, British Columbia. Retrieved from University of British Columbia Library, DOI: 10.14288/1.0132754.

49. AMA Ed Hub. "Get Rid of Stupid Stuff: Reduce the Unnecessary Daily Burdens for Clinicians." AMA Ed Hub. Published December 19, 2019. https://edhub.ama-assn.org/steps-forward/module/2757858.

50. University of Houston. n.d. *CoogsCARE: Supporting Mental Health and Wellness.* https://www.uh.edu/coogs-care/index.php.

51. Humphrey, Albert S. 2005. "SWOT Analysis." *Long Range Planning* 30 (1): 46–52. https://theapprenticeshartpury.wordpress.com/2015/02/15/swot-analysis/.

52. Weaver, Liz. 2015. "Turf, Trust and the Collaboration Spectrum." *Collective Impact Forum*, March 19, 2015. https://collectiveimpactforum.org/blog/turf-trust-and-the-collaboration-spectrum/.

53. Weaver, Liz. 2021. "The Collaboration Spectrum Revisited." The Collaboration Spectrum. Image from PDF. https://www.tamarackcommunity.ca/hubfs/Resources/Publications/Collaboration%20Spectrum%20Revisited_Liz%20Weaver.pdf.

54. W.K. Kellogg Foundation. 2004. *Logic Model Development Guide.* January 1, 2004. https://wkkf.issuelab.org/resource/logic-model-development-guide.html.

55. HERO (Health Enhancement Research Organization). n.d. *HERO Health and Well-being Best Practices Scorecard in Collaboration with Mercer© (HERO Scorecard).* https://hero-health.org/hero-scorecard/.

56. Oklahoma State Department of Health. n.d. *Certified Healthy Oklahoma.* https://oklahoma.gov/certifiedhealthy.html.

57. Lynch, Wendy. 2021. *Become an Analytic Translator: Make Sense of Data in Business. Make Allies of Analysts and Business Leaders.* CreateSpace Independent Publishing.

THANK YOU

Dear Reader,

Thank you for reading my book. My intention was to share a snapshot in time with the hope of providing a useful model that can help you grow and evolve in your well-being role—even as life keeps going and new lessons in well-being emerge every day. You have wisdom to contribute too—especially in a field as dynamic as well-being. That's part of the beauty: well-being evolves, and so do we.

To keep the conversation going, I've built a dynamic home at **www.SuzyHarrington.com**. My aim is for the site to serve as a living resource where we can share insights, and you can browse an expanding library of tools and explore a customizable, portable version of the model that you can adapt for your own organization. I plan to share updates and new ideas as our collective knowledge grows.

You'll also find a downloadable PDF workbook with the exercises from this book on my website. Because, as much as we scribble in the margins, there's never quite enough room—and shared learning keeps this work alive.

To your thriving well-being initiatives and success,

— **Suzy**

www.ingramcontent.com/pod-product-compliance
Lightning Source LLC
Chambersburg PA
CBHW060515080526
44586CB00012B/497